Endorsements for
Fresh Bread

Fresh Bread is perhaps the best I have found relating to the Lord's Prayer. Not only does Michael do an astute job of peeling off the outward layers of the Lord's Prayer to reveal the deeper, hidden insights therein, but the key in this particular writing that activated and engaged my Spirit was how he helped to illuminate the reality that each individual element included in the tapestry of the Lord's Prayer contains the careful and intentional weaving of our identity and the identity of our Creator. As a reader, you cannot help but to be provoked and encouraged to live out the unique identity and purpose for which you were created!
Kyle Koch, lead pastor, The Movement, Indiana

In *Fresh Bread*, I was immediately drawn to chapter 9, "And Do Not Lead Us into Temptation," because I have always struggled with that verse. The explanation presented flows smoothly and is refreshing. The summary is the best I've ever heard and rings so clearly, like a bell on a cold winter's night. I now understand what Jesus was saying in that verse. Thank you, Michael!
Steve Wells, businessman, Michigan

Fresh Bread by Michael French is a well-written, engaging book that probes deeper into the greatest model for prayer we have in scripture—the Lord's

Prayer. In a time when the Church at large desperately needs to be more involved in prayer, this book lays a wonderful foundation and blueprint. It presents each section of the prayer in careful and thought-provoking chapters. Michael skillfully describes the meanings of each section, drawing out revelation from what was meant in the original text and what the ancients knew. I firmly believe that *Fresh Bread* will be a great tool in training up a new generation of prayer warriors while drawing hearts closer to Him.
Shawn Lombard, Harbinger Song Ministries, Alabama

Fresh Bread is a perfect title for this book. Every sense is touched by this analogy. Michael's outlook on the Lord's Prayer opens a new perspective on what it meant when the disciples said, "Teach us to pray." Even if you have read other works on the topic, this book will take you to new depths of understanding.
Arthur Hernandez, founder, Bridge Kauai, Hawaii

The more I got into *Fresh Bread*, the more I enjoyed and benefited from it. Thank you, Michael French! I believe it is an excellent book, not just for individuals, but also for small groups to do a chapter a week.
Tony Cooke, director, Streams Training Center, England

Fresh Bread:
Finding Your Daily Portion in the Lord's Prayer
Michael B. French
Copyright @ 2016 ShadeTree Publishing, LLC
Print ISBN: 978-1-937331-86-3
e-Book ISBN: 978-1-937331-87-0

Scripture quotations are taken from the King James Version, which is public domain in the United States.

Scripture quotations marked "ESV" are taken from the The ESV® Bible (The Holy Bible, English Standard Version®). ESV® Permanent Text Edition® (2016). Copyright © 2001 by Crossway, a publishing ministry of Good News Publishers. The ESV® text has been reproduced in cooperation with and by permission of Good News Publishers. Unauthorized reproduction of this publication is prohibited. All rights reserved.

Scripture quotations marked "NIV" are taken from THE HOLY BIBLE, NEW INTERNATIONAL VERSION®, NIV® Copyright © 1973, 1978, 1984, 2011 by Biblica, Inc.® Used by permission. All rights reserved worldwide.

Scripture quotations marked "NKJV" are taken from the New King James Version®. Copyright © 1982 by Thomas Nelson, Inc. All rights reserved.

Scripture quotations marked "TLB" are taken from The Living Bible copyright © 1971 by Tyndale House Foundation. Used by permission of Tyndale House Publishers Inc., Carol Stream, Illinois 60188. All rights reserved. The Living Bible, TLB, and the The Living Bible logo are registered trademarks of Tyndale House Publishers.

Scripture quotations marked "AMPC" are taken from the Amplified® Bible (AMPC), Copyright © 1954, 1958, 1962, 1964, 1965, 1987 by The Lockman Foundation Used by permission. www.Lockman.org"

Scripture quotations marked "ASV" are taken from the American Standard Version. The ASV is public domain in the United States.

Scripture quotations marked "RSV" are taken from the Revised Standard Version of the Bible, copyright © 1946, 1952, and 1971 the Division of Christian Education of the National Council of the Churches of Christ in the United States of America. Used by permission. All rights reserved.

Cover image created with images used under license from DerekHatfield/Shutterstock.com and SvetlanaLukienko/Shutterstock.com. Other images used under license from ©kseniavasil/Fotolia and purchased from Andy Robinson.

All rights reserved. This book is protected by copyright. No part of this book may be reproduced or transmitted in any form or by any means, electronic or mechanical, including photocopying, recording, or by any information storage and retrieval system, without permission in writing from the publisher.

The purpose of this book is to educate and enlighten. This book is sold with the understanding that the publisher and author are not engaged in rendering counseling, albeit it professional or lay, to the reader or anyone else. The author shall have neither liability nor responsibility to any person or entity with respect to any loss or damage caused, or alleged to have been caused, directly or indirectly, by the information contain in this book.

Visit our Web site at www.ShadeTreePublishing.com.

Contents

Foreword 1
Introduction 3
Chapter 1 Our Father 9
Chapter 2 Who Art in Heaven 25
Chapter 3 Hallowed Be Your Name 35
Chapter 4 Your Kingdom Come 49
Chapter 5 Your Will Be Done 67
Chapter 6 On Earth As It Is in Heaven 79
Chapter 7 Give Us This Day Our Daily Bread 91
Chapter 8 Forgive Us Our Debts, As We Forgive Our Debtors 107
Chapter 9 Lead Us Not into Temptation 123
Chapter 10 But Deliver Us from Evil 135
Chapter 11 Kingdom, Power, and Glory 147
Chapter 12 Amen 157
Conclusion 163
Review Request 167
About the Author 168
Other Books by Michael B. French 169
About Patria Ministries 171
Acknowledgments 173
Scriptures and References 175

Dedication

Between the time I began writing this book and the time I finished it, my life changed in what feels like an unimaginable way. On my fiftieth birthday, I lost one of my dearest friends and a personal spiritual father, John Paul Jackson. Four months later, I lost my other spiritual father, Bill French, who was also my earthly father. As I wrote the final words of this book, I was overwhelmed with emotions. The opening words of the Lord's Prayer, "Our Father," took on a whole new meaning to me. While considering the influence and monumental impact that these two earthly men had upon my life as "fathers," I realized that my understanding of "our Father," God, has been, and perhaps always will be, far too shallow. In different ways, these two men molded me into who I am today. They were good reflections of my heavenly Father, and for that I will be eternally grateful. Much of what I have written in these pages and much of my understanding of my relationship with God as expressed through the Lord's Prayer was imparted to me through the lives of John Paul and my dad. For this reason, I dedicate this book to these two great men, and by writing it, I hope that it in some way says "thank you!"

Foreword

by Jason Hooper
Senior Pastor of King's Way Church
Birmingham, Alabama

Fresh Bread by Michael B. French is more than a book on prayer or a guideline showing *how* to pray or even a manual on *why* we should pray. Instead, *Fresh Bread* is an invitation—an invitation to embark on a journey of intimacy that unlocks divine destiny and awakens true Kingdom perspective, empowering you to live and grow with God as you become all that He has created you to be while releasing the fullness of heaven here on earth.

I give my highest endorsement to *Fresh Bread* and encourage you as a reader to take your time with this book, allowing the Holy Spirit to breathe upon the truth of these written words in such a way that they would become a living word in your life. As you take your seat at His table, allow Him to bless and break open this *Fresh Bread* in a way that invites you to draw near to God, moving beyond knowing about the Lord to knowing Him in a real and tangible way.

Fresh Bread by Michael B. French

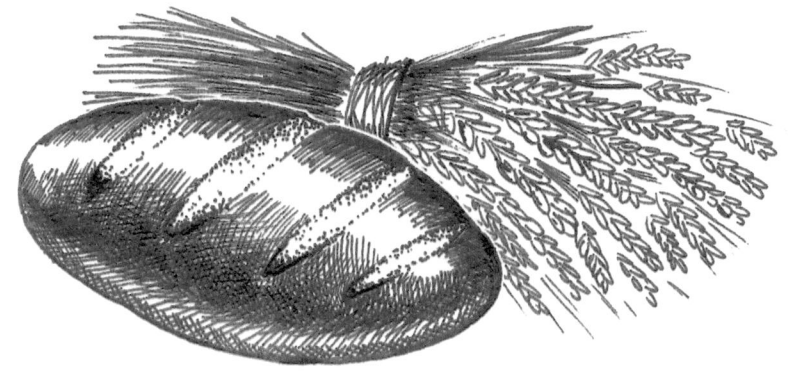

Introduction

Have you ever traveled through the part of town where a bakery was in operation or come home just as your mother pulled a loaf of homemade bread from the oven? If so, then you have had the enjoyment of one of my favorite sensory experiences—the aroma of fresh bread wafting through the room and changing the atmosphere. It's not that last week's loaf isn't just as nutritional or every bit as good for our meal, but rather that an extra tidbit of joy comes from experiencing the sight, smell, and flavor of the bread in a fresh, new way.

Certainly there is something to be said for the goodness and consistency of the loaf waiting for us in the bread box. We go to great pains to preserve it and have it available at a moment's notice. So, it isn't the idea of something completely new that is appealing, but rather the opportunity to experience something old in a fresh, new way. Maybe this is what the author of Ecclesiastes was thinking when he wrote, "That which has been is what will be, that which is done is what will be done, and there is nothing new under the sun."[1] After all, the recipe for the bread isn't what changed; instead, it is the environment in which we are experiencing the finished product that has shifted. The bread itself hasn't changed; it remains just what it has always been—a staple of our diet. What we do to bake bread hasn't changed in centuries or even millennia. Though the specific means may have improved, we still bake it just the same. Bread is certainly nothing new, but that doesn't mean our experience can't be new every time a loaf is pulled from the oven.

The Lord's Prayer is not new. In fact, it is an ancient prayer, and neither its recipe nor its value has changed over the course of time. On the other hand, viewing it from a different vantage point can increase the opportunity for us to experience it fresh each time we pray. It is from this perspective that I want us to examine the Lord's Prayer together. The Lord once spoke to Jeremiah and instructed him to say, "Stand in the ways and see, and ask for the old paths, where the good way is, and walk in it; Then you will find rest for your souls."[2] Unfortunately for those hearing Jeremiah's words, they answered, "We will not walk in it." Unlike the people of Jeremiah's day, we can press forward into the path with an understanding that old things don't have to stay old—they can become new, just as Paul spoke of concerning our lives in Christ.[3] We may be asking for the old path when we pray the Lord's Prayer, but the value has never faded and it is time for us to begin to search that path to find the rest for our souls that it provides.

Some will argue that the Lord's Prayer is a traditional prayer that has no place of real value in the contemporary church. Others will say that it is nothing more than an outline of topics about which we should be praying. A few will recognize that when Jesus used it to teach His disciples, as with most of His teaching, there was probably far more to be understood than what first meets the eye. In any event, the Lord's Prayer is likely the most recognizable prayer of the Christian faith, repeated not only at churches, but at sporting and social events, in times of joy and crisis, and by people of every race and tribe. This prayer is ingrained in the minds of those who make up the body of Christ around the world and, to some extent, even in those who don't.

The words of this prayer have been repeated throughout the generations by people from virtually every culture and in almost every language. Yet when Jesus chose to describe prayer in this way, He was not giving us a chant to recite, like the mantras of Eastern religions, nor was He providing us with an easily memorized poetic prayer that lends itself to ritualistic repetition. Instead, He was inviting us to go deeper in our relationship with the God to whom we are praying—to make our prayer more than mere words. He was offering us an outline that would focus our attention on the things that mattered to God.

Many prayers have been written to help us remember key points or even simply to help remind us to pray. Some of our earliest childhood memories may actually be found in the words of one of those types of prayer: "Now I lay me down to sleep, I pray the Lord my soul to keep. If I should die before I wake, I pray the Lord my soul to take." There is certainly nothing wrong with the use of this eighteenth-century children's prayer, but for thousands of individuals, this prayer and the Lord's Prayer have one key component in common: They are both filled with habitual phrases used in a routine fashion at specific times to produce comfort out of familiarity. It is my hope that by more closely examining the purpose and the message behind the words of the Lord's Prayer, we can stop it from spiraling into obscurity and recognize it as more than a relic to be set upon a shelf and admired from time to time.

Like it also does for a fine wine, age has only added to the richness of this mighty prayer. Two thousand years ago, Jesus communicated deep truths to His disciples through these words. A somewhat modern understanding of the prayer has taught us that it is not actually the Lord's Prayer at all. That is, it is not a prayer that the Lord prayed as much as it is a teaching on prayer for His disciples. Perhaps it could more aptly be called the Disciples' Prayer. Travel down the ancient path involves memorizing the words and being able to use them as a form of prayer, but smelling the fresh bread involves grasping the meaning of those same words and then understanding what Jesus was teaching us about both prayer itself and what we should be praying for.

In searching out the old path, the foundational understanding of the prayer Jesus used to teach His disciples how to pray, we will find a good way in which to walk. As we learn to understand the freshness of this ancient road map, we will find a place of rest for our souls. The question is not whether there is value in the words themselves (of course there is), but rather whether we will take the time to smell the aroma of the fresh bread and "taste and see that the Lord is good"[4] as we delve into the depth of those words.

> *In this manner, therefore, pray:*
> *Our Father in heaven, hallowed be Your name. Your kingdom come. Your will be done on earth as it is in heaven. Give us this day our daily bread. And forgive us our debts, as we forgive our debtors. And do not lead us into temptation, but deliver us from the evil one. For Yours is the kingdom and the power and the glory forever. Amen.*
> Matthew 6:9–13 NKJV

Breathe deeply and take in the aroma of fresh bread as we begin our journey through these revered words of the Lord's Prayer. Don't get in a rush to finish praying with some old-fashioned mind-set or by simply using repetitious language. Instead, savor every word and let the "taste" of them linger upon your lips as you experience this living bread from heaven and allow it to change your prayer life forever.

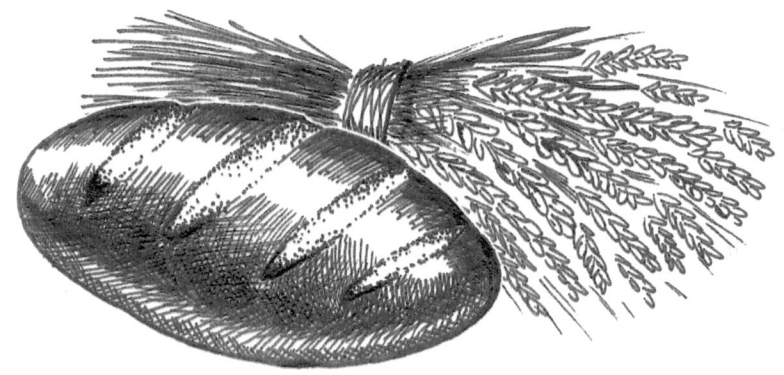

Chapter 1
Our Father

Think about the imagery released by just the first two words of the Lord's Prayer—"Our Father." Did you ever stop to imagine or experience God as more than some all-powerful being who created the universe? Take the time to be still and know Him as a Father.

Of course, the image of God as the omnipotent, omniscient, omnipresent Creator is amazing and helps us to understand just how big He really is, but it is equally important to recognize just how loving and personal God is. Jesus chose to teach us to open up our prayer with words that would help us recognize the latter and understand who it is we are talking to, not just what He is.

The very nature of this salutation should help to point us away from the ritualistic way the prayer has been used, and toward a recognition that it should be a personal conversation. Instead, for far too long the Church has actually failed to realize the depth of relationship that this phrase brings to the words that follow. Truly knowing who we are addressing can radically change the way we communicate with Him. Jesus was teaching us that prayer is real, personal communication with Someone who is more than a creator. He was pointing out to us that we have the opportunity to talk directly to our dad.

Particularly in Western culture, we have, over time, taken to opening our prayers in a formal way, the most common of which may be "Dear Lord." Consider the difference between this common opening and the way Jesus opened the Lord's Prayer. The term *father* conveys the idea of parenthood and indicates that we can talk to God in the same way we would talk to our natural father. On the other hand, the term *Lord* conveys the idea of aristocracy and indicates that we might talk to God in the same manner that a servant would address his master. This salutation is perhaps at the heart of the difficulty that some individuals have in expressing themselves in prayer. Even many who open their prayer as a conversation with their father tend to formalize their language with words like "Dear heavenly Father," with the emphasis being on *heavenly*, which distances God from them rather than recognizes His closeness. Have the words we have chosen to open our prayers distanced us from "our Father," or has distance from "our Father" affected the words we have chosen to open our prayers? In either case, we seem to have drifted from a real understanding of whom we are addressing in prayer.

A Father to Us

Jesus made prayer personal by teaching us it should be addressed to "Father" God. Moreover, He also assured us that we are not merely praying to a father, but that we are praying to "our" Father. Consider the fact that not everyone has this privilege—in other words, not everyone recognizes Him as Father in the way that the term is used here. Certainly He is the Creator of every living thing, but there are those individuals to whom He is not Father, because some of His creation has rejected Him. The Greek term used here is *pater* (pat-ayr'), and while it can be used to describe the founder of a race or tribe, one advanced in years, or even the Creator of all intelligent beings, its deeper meaning speaks more literally of a nourisher, protector, and upholder.[5] Jesus put it this way on one occasion as He spoke to the Pharisees:

> *Jesus said to them, "If God were your Father, you would love me, for I came from God and I am here. I came not of my own accord, but he sent me. Why do you not understand what I say? It is because you cannot bear to hear my word. You are of*

> *your father the devil, and your will is to do your father's desires. He was a murderer from the beginning, and has nothing to do with the truth, because there is no truth in him. When he lies, he speaks out of his own character, for he is a liar and the father of lies. But because I tell the truth, you do not believe me."*
>
> John 8:42–45 ESV

Is it any wonder that the Lord's Prayer would begin with a reminder that God is "our Father," when the Pharisees, perhaps the most important religious leaders of that time, did not understand their relationship with God? This is a powerful reminder that our spiritual DNA changes when we come to understand our true relationship with God. Jesus told Nicodemus in John 3 that no one could see the Kingdom of God unless they were "born again." When Jesus spoke these words and John wrote them down, the language used was specifically chosen to be ambiguous, as the Greek wording can mean either "born again" or "born from above."[6] While Jesus was clearly using a metaphor, it seems as though it is quite possible that He also wanted us to understand that the spiritual experience He was describing was quite literal. While our salvation experience is spiritual, and when we are saved we are metaphorically born into the Kingdom of heaven, we are also re-conceived as if we had returned to the womb and begun life anew—

no longer fathered by that liar, the devil, but by the Spirit of Truth Himself.

This understanding that we have been re-conceived is why Paul can say that those who are in Christ are a new creation, that old things (like who our father was) have passed away and that all things (like who our Father now is) have become new.[7] When it comes to addressing God in prayer, there is a very real distinction between those who have accepted Jesus Christ as their Savior and those who have not.

We don't address God as our Father just because He is our Creator, but because He really has become our Father in all the ways the synonyms of that word convey. He is *Dad*, *Daddy*, and *Papa* to us. While the dictionary definition of these words may appear little different from that of the word *father*, they carry and convey something more. There is an emotional attachment connected with these names of endearment. A natural father is a part of the creative process that results in the lives of his children. In that same sense, God is our Creator. However, when the term "our" is added, as it is here in this beautiful prayer, something changes and He becomes more personal than just a Creator. While "dad" is also recognized as describing the same person, he becomes more personal. He is there for the kids, he participates in their lives, he goes to their ball games, and he weeps with their pain and laughs with their joy. Opening the Lord's Prayer with the phrase "Our Father" was the cultural equivalent of affectionately saying, "Hey, Dad."

The Father of All

While those who do not love Jesus may have rejected God as their Father, it is important to note that He has not rejected them. He cares for His creation, His children, whether they deserve it or not, and each of us should be grateful for that fact. Clearly we have all lived our lives in such a way that there was some point at which we didn't recognize God as our Father, even though He still was. Here, in these opening words of the Lord's Prayer, we are not only being taught how personal our relationship to God really is, but we are being reminded that God loved us before we understood this. As a result of that understanding, it becomes apparent that Jesus was also reminding us of our responsibility to those who don't yet know God as their Father. After all, if God loves them and considers them His children even when they don't recognize Him, is it really our place to reject and condemn them? The way Jesus explained it, our ability to love them is part of what helps us understand the Father/child relationship we have with God. In Matthew 5, Jesus commanded us to love our enemies, to bless those who curse us, to do good to those who hate us, and to pray for those who persecute us. In so doing, He said we become sons of our Father in heaven.[8]

Matthew 5:45 goes on to explain that God, our Father, makes His sun rise and His rain fall on both the just and the unjust. When we truly understand that the God to whom we are praying is our Father, then we must accept that we have brothers and sisters—some of whom also know Him as Father and others who do not. In most natural families the members don't pick and choose whom they love based upon whether or not they are doing everything right, but rather, they love them because they are part of the family. In this same way, Jesus says we cannot just love those who love us, but rather we need to be like our Father and love even those who don't love us.[9] After all, "God so loved the world, that he gave his only Son, that whoever believes in Him should not perish but have eternal life."[10] We have a responsibility to those around us, whether they are just or unjust. It is not based upon how they treat us, it is not based upon how we feel about them, it is not based upon what they say to us, it is not based upon the way they look; rather, it is based upon the fact that God loves them. If He really is our Father, then we have a responsibility to love them too.

Jesus taught us that we must love our neighbors (both those born again and those not) as ourselves.[11] John would later go on to explain that we cannot love God, whom we have not seen, if we cannot love those around us whom we have seen.[12] Our conversation with God should be an expression of our love for our Father, and understanding how much He loves those around us, then loving them as He does, deepens our relationship to Him and our communication with Him.

It is also important to recognize when we pray that not one of us has a monopoly on God. While He certainly is my Father, He is not mine alone. He has a lot of children, and He cares for each of us individually. There are still some large families today, but only a few generations ago it was not uncommon to see a family of ten to twelve children. With a family that size, no one child could claim their parents' full attention, but Dad would still be everyone's dad. The amazing thing about God is that He has the capacity to treat us like an only child and yet we are still each part of a much larger family. Each of us individually can go to our Father and still receive the special treatment afforded by having Him as Father. Just like it is in those big natural families, where any of the kids can climb up into Daddy's lap and become the focus of his attention, we have that same opportunity with God every time we cry out to Him in prayer.

The Hebrew View

In the Hebrew culture and the mind-set of a Jew at the time Jesus lived, the father was the most important figure in the household. They recognized not only the father in the household, but the generational fathers. Remember, God was known as the God of Abraham, Isaac, and Jacob. These were fathers of the faith—fathers who had raised up generations of both natural and spiritual children. They recognized fathers like Elijah, who was able to train up his spiritual son, Elisha, to receive a double portion. Both these generational fathers and those in individual households were due honor and respect, not only because they were loving and kind to their children, but also because they were strong and willing to discipline when it was needed. So, when Jesus directed His prayer to the Father, He wasn't relating to what our personal family experience might be, but rather to what it meant within the Hebrew culture to be a father.

We sometimes look at God in the way our own culture has taught us to look at a father. Unfortunately, our culture has taught us that a father should never do anything to disappoint a child. It has also taught us that fathers should not discipline their children because it might result in their self-esteem being damaged. As a result, we sometimes pray expecting God to answer us and give us what we want, simply because we are His children, rather than understanding that as a good Father He will do what is best for us and for our destiny. Somehow our cultural mind-set has led us to expect that everything God gives us will always feel good. This simply is not the type of father to whom Jesus taught us to pray. Jesus was speaking to a culture that valued and understood the role of the natural father and acknowledged that this was the way the disciples could relate to God. God loves us and He wants to give good gifts to us, because He is our Father.[13] However, He is not afraid to keep us in order, and He will not hold back from correcting us and keeping us on track to become a success in Kingdom life.

And have you forgotten the exhortation that addresses you as sons? "My son, do not regard lightly the discipline of the Lord, nor be weary when reproved by him. For the Lord disciplines the one he loves, and chastises every son whom he receives." It is for discipline that you have to endure. God is treating you as sons. For what son is there whom his father does not discipline? If you are left without discipline, in which all have participated, then you are illegitimate children and not sons.

Hebrews 12:5–9 ESV

God is a Father who wants good things for His children, but when we pray to Him as Father, we have to remember that, more than He wants good things for us, He desires to be a good Father to us. He doesn't just give us everything we want. If a child wants to place his finger into an electrical socket, no good earthly father will let him do it just because he wants to. In the same way, our Father God knows that some of the things we think are fun really aren't good for us, so when He disciplines us, it is not a bad thing. By correcting us, He doesn't cause us to lose something; He causes us to gain something. Right from the start, Jesus is establishing the principle that we can't say to God, "You don't love me because You didn't answer me the way I wanted." Our Father loves us too much to give us anything that would be harmful to us, and He knows more than we do, because He sees the end from the beginning. Earthly fathers may not have the luxury of knowing all these things, but an omniscient God does.

How many times have we prayed to God and then dishonored Him when He did not give us what we wanted? To do so indicates that we don't know whom we are talking to. Malachi received a word from the Lord regarding the honor due to a father:

> *A son honors his father, and a servant his master. If then I am a father, where is my honor? And if I am a master, where is my fear? says the Lord of hosts to you, O priests, who despise my name. But you say, "How have we despised your name?"*
>
> Malachi 1:6 ESV

When we address our prayers to our Father, we open the door to a personal prayer life, but it equally imparts obligations that we must fulfill. If we are to pray to God as Father, then we must respect Him enough to do more than just get by. The priests of Malachi's day were technically doing their jobs, but they were only offering their second best—and God called their bluff. When we call God our Father, we have an obligation to give Him our best. He wants the best for us. He sees the best in us. He expects us to give our best. What natural father would train up their child and say, "Now, go out there and give me a second-place effort!" Dare we expect any less from God?

It is important that we remember our prayer is made to God, our Father. When we pray, we must remember all that this concept includes. Let us not forget that our spiritual DNA has changed. This means that we have privileges and responsibilities that those who don't know Him as Father do not have.

> *No one born of God makes a practice of sinning, for God's seed abides in him, and he cannot keep on sinning because he has been born of God. By this it is evident who are the children of God, and who are the children of the devil: whoever does not practice righteousness is not of God, nor is the one who does not love his brother.*
>
> 1 John 3:9–10 ESV

The Greek word translated "seed" here is the word *sperma*,[14] and it means that the seed, or sperm, of God abides in us. We have God's DNA. When we say we are born again, we sometimes fail to realize how powerful that statement is. We have literally been re-created spiritually speaking, born again to a new Dad and His DNA remains in us. By teaching us the Lord's Prayer, Jesus acknowledged that we could pray to God as a son!

"Our Father"—to the One who is more than a detached Creator, but a personal and intimate parent. It is to You that we open our mouths and cry out. Before we even knew You, You loved us and fathered us. It is to You, the most important figure in our lives, that we pray.

Breaking Bread

Our Father
(Matthew 6:9a)

EXAMINE

Jesus opens this prayer by addressing God as a Father. How do you typically open the lines of communication with God? Why?

_____

_____

_____

_____

Describe your relationship with your natural father. How has this affected your relationship with your heavenly Father? Consider 1 John 4:20 in your answer.

_____

_____

_____

Does recognizing God as a Father change the way you pray? In what ways?

The way God answers prayer is often categorized as yes, no, or wait. Does recognizing God as "Our Father" provide any insight into the way God responds? Explain your answer.

Spiritually speaking, our DNA changes when we are born again and we are literally re-conceived. How does this impact our prayer life and our overall Christian walk? Consider 1 John 3:9–10 in your answer.

_____

_____

_____

REFLECT

Take some time this week to meditate on the phrase "Our Father" from Matthew 6:9. Release any preconceived ideas of what a father is or should be and ask God to reveal Himself to you as your Father in a personal way. Set aside at least fifteen minutes to spend just being quiet and listening.

ACT

Make a list of at least five positive characteristics that you identify with a good father. Write a short testimony of how God has exemplified each those characteristics in your own life.

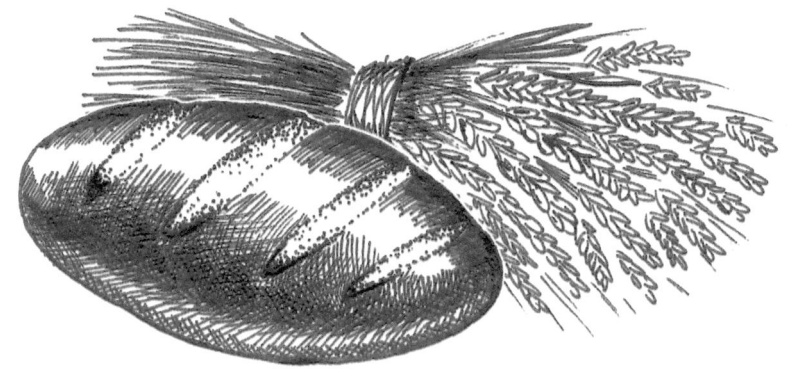

Chapter 2
Who Art in Heaven

We serve a supernatural God. He is not merely a man, but rather He is the Creator of men. He may be our Father, but His abode is not upon the earth that He created, but "in heaven."

> *Thus says the Lord: "Heaven is my throne, and the earth is my footstool; what is the house that you would build for me, and what is the place of my rest?"*
>
> Isaiah 66:1 ESV

Isaiah 66 reminds us that He is a King—for it is a king who sits upon a throne. And He is not just any king, but He is the King of all kings and He reigns from

His throne in heaven. This Ruler of the universe is the very same One who, as we have already been reminded, desires to relate to us as a father. The second verse of Isaiah 66 goes on to instruct us that Creator God is willing to spend time with His creation and look upon those who are "humble and contrite in spirit and trembles at [His] word." Do we realize what Jesus was suggesting when He taught the disciples to think in this way when they were praying? When we pray to our Father in heaven, we are recognizing our personal connection to Him and acknowledging His authority over us.

The Creator of the universe has established His Kingdom in a place called heaven. It is there that His throne is positioned, and it is from there that He rules. This simple addition to the phrase "our Father" is a reminder that God is personal and close to us, but that does not mean we can comprehend Him simply. He is still the Creator of all things. This God, who exists beyond space and time, loved us enough to enter the earth so that His children could have a sense of relationship with Him. He cared enough to come to the earth, make Himself like one of us, and give up His life so that this relationship could be sealed and reestablished. If the phrase "our Father" conveys the sense of a deep personal relationship, then "in heaven" conveys the idea of wonder in a God who is incomprehensible in His majesty.

God's throne is in heaven, but His footstool is on the earth. If the throne conveys the authority of God, then the footstool conveys the rest that is derived from relationship with Him. Consider the words of Genesis as it describes God's initial interaction with His creation. By the time of the Fall, Adam had come to expect and listen for the sound of God walking in the Garden at the cool of the day.[15] God Himself would leave His throne in heaven and place His feet on the footstool of the earth in order to spend time with His children. God, who reigned in heaven, would listen to Adam and Eve and converse with them. As long as they trembled at His voice (obeyed His commands), they had this privilege. When we come to God in prayer, we come to Him as a Father who is due our love and respect, but we also come to Him as a King who is due our honor and obedience.

The most significant consequence that resulted from Adam being removed from the Garden was not that he now had to work to till the ground, but rather that the relationship with his Father was damaged and he had to work to restore it. The earth would still produce food, through the toil of Adam's hands, but this relational consequence was insurmountable by man, no matter how hard he worked. God would still be in heaven, but the interaction of our Father in heaven with man on the earth was limited. Jesus said to pray like this: "Our Father in heaven," because He knew He was going to die and rise again to restore that relationship. The God of heaven was once again going to walk and talk with His children. Though we are still praying to God, who is in heaven, Jesus' sacrifice eliminated the veil that had been drawn to separate man from Him.

When we consider that the abode of God is in heaven, we are reminded of just how big He is and just how amazing it is that He has chosen us. However, there is still something more here. To put it more directly, when we read these words, we can't help but stop and ask the question—"Where is heaven?"

Somewhere Out There?
We tend to think of heaven as some supernatural place that exists somewhere out beyond the stars. Hell, of course, is found in the center of the earth (an image reinforced by the scientific discovery that the earth does, indeed, have a molten core). The truth is that we really don't understand heaven and hell, nor do we comprehend where they are located, at least not from a true biblical perspective. In truth, it is probably much more appropriate to consider heaven as a different dimension than it is to think of it as a specific place beyond the stars. This may sound ridiculous until we consider it more closely. Which seems more feasible: that we could build a spaceship and launch out somewhere beyond the last visible star and actually reach heaven, or that we could simply step across an invisible boundary and into another dimension that is heaven? Heaven is not "somewhere out there," but rather it is close to us and all around us. Yet again our amazing Creator is close enough to be called "Father," and He is near enough for us to have access to Him at any time.

We cannot pray in the manner that Jesus instructed us to unless and until we recognize that our relationship with the God of heaven has been restored. Remember that the throne of God, which is found in heaven according to Isaiah, is representative of His Kingdom. With this in mind, consider the question asked of Jesus by the Pharisees when they sought to know when the Kingdom of God would be seen:

> *Now when He was asked by the Pharisees when the kingdom of God would come, He answered them and said, "The kingdom of God does not come with observation; nor will they say, 'See here!' or 'See there!' For indeed, the kingdom of God is within you."*
>
> Luke 17:20–21 NKJV

According to Jesus, the Kingdom of God is not something we look out beyond the stars to find, but rather it is within us. Jesus was saying, "God dwells within you." Everything we think of as heaven is there—in us—when our relationship is restored. Where is heaven? It is within us. "Do you not know that your body is the temple of the Holy Spirit?"[16] The throne of God resides inside of us. Heaven is not somewhere out there. God dwells in us! We expect to receive health and life, provision and resources, wisdom and understanding, when we reach heaven someday in the distant future. Yet in these very opening words of the Lord's Prayer, Jesus is teaching us that God is closer than we think and that all the resources of heaven are not waiting in some distant place at some distant time, but rather are available here and now. When we begin to pray like Jesus explains, heaven is moved out of the distance and into our lives. When this happens, our Father in heaven once again places His feet upon the earth through us.

At times, we try to envision God out there somewhere looking down on us, yet the truth is that He is right here, experiencing life with us. The works we do, the lives we live, the ways we demonstrate character, integrity, humility, and righteousness, what we display before man—all allow God to be glorified in us.

> *In the same way, let your light shine before others, so that they may see your good works and give glory to your Father who is in heaven.*
>
> Matthew 5:16 ESV

Everything that Jesus is going to explain about prayer is summed up in these first four words: "our Father in heaven." Everything that comes after this is an expression of what has already been declared here.

Consider the level of honor and respect that is due God when we truly understand Him. He, the Creator of everything and whose throne is in heaven and whose footstool is the earth, is willing to walk and talk with man and build a relationship with him. When Jesus teaches us to pray to "our Father in heaven," He is not suggesting that we need to shout to a God who is distant from us, but rather that we communicate with a Father who loves us enough to humble Himself and come have communion with us. Jesus came to restore what was lost in the Garden. He is instructing us to get back to the relationship with our Father that Adam once had and see heaven once again move into the earth. In this way, prayer becomes more than a string of words tied together, and instead establishes a personal relationship with our Creator.

"Who art in heaven." Though You are the Creator of the universe, You are not distant from us. We are awed by Your incomprehensible majesty and the fact that You would draw back the veil between heaven and earth and allow us to be a part of what You are doing. We love You as our Father, and we honor You as our Creator and King.

Fresh Bread by Michael B. French

Breaking Bread

Who Art in Heaven
(Matthew 6:9b)

EXAMINE

When you think about heaven, where do you consider it to be located? Why?

___

___

___

___

Isaiah 66:1 describes heaven as a thing (a throne) rather than a location. Why is this important, and what does it reveal about heaven?

___

___

___

___

Does understanding what heaven is and where it is located help you to better understand your relationship with God? Why or why not?

___

___

___

___

REFLECT

Take some time this week to meditate on the phrase "in heaven" from Matthew 6:9. Reflect on how your life is transformed by having the Kingdom of God inside of you (Luke 17:20–21) and what that means to the way you approach each day. Set aside at least fifteen minutes to spend just being quiet and listening.

ACT

Find a comfortable chair and something that could serve as a footstool. Take a seat in the chair (metaphorically considering it to be your throne), then stretch out your legs and let them rest on the footstool. Make a list of at least five things that describe your position and your relationship to the throne and the footstool. Then write a short paragraph describing the relationship between heaven and earth based upon your observations.

Fresh Bread by Michael B. French

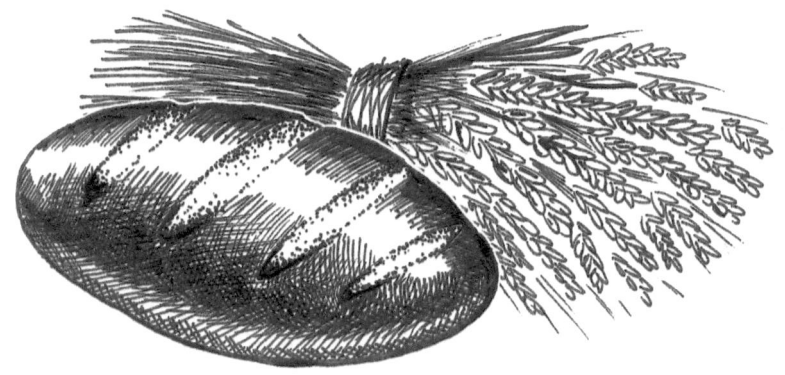

Chapter 3
Hallowed Be Your Name

Now that we have a deeper appreciation for whom we are addressing in prayer, we can consider our initial response to this majestic King who calls us His children. Perhaps the phrase, "hallowed be Your name" is simply an expression of praise, but if we can appreciate the complexity of Jesus' teachings as He expressed Himself through simple language, we will find it to be something much, much more.

To "Hallow"
The English term to *hallow* means "to make holy" or "to set apart as sacred," and thus the idea that this portion of the prayer is an expression intended to

praise the name of the Lord and honor Him as holy is quite logical. To stop here, however, forgets that the logic of man and the logic of God are quite different. Remember, Isaiah 55:9 reminds us that God's ways and thoughts are higher than ours. In the original language from which this passage is translated, we find that it might be more accurate to read the passage as "our Father in heaven, make Your name holy!"

This phrase is not merely a declaration of praise for the King of heaven, but rather a petition or a plea that God would sanctify His name in the earth. If the God of heaven is going to place His feet upon the earth and walk with man again, then we should recognize that we, as men and women, are incapable of fully giving Him what He is due, and as such, should be petitioning Him to make His own ame holy in the earth. Clearly, the Word of God teaches us that we ought to give praise to the Lord and that it is part of our responsibility to magnify His name, but what we can offer on our own is insufficient and needs to be infused with the power of His presence so that His name and His holiness might be fully comprehended.

In the minds of the Hebrew people, the idea of holiness was equated with sanctification, yet even that idea was too difficult to define in a concrete fashion. Most frequently it was simply thought of in terms of the ability to understand its opposite—to profane. Under the Old Covenant, God's name could either be profaned or it could be made holy. The goal of the

Jewish people and the commandment given to Israel was to keep His name from becoming profane.

> *So you shall keep my commandments and do them: I am the Lord. And you shall not profane my holy name, that I may be sanctified among the people of Israel. I am the Lord who sanctifies you, who brought you out of the land of Egypt to be your God: I am the Lord.*
>
> Leviticus 22:31–33 ESV

If you are reading this book and you are a Christian, then it is highly unlikely that you would ever even consider actively profaning the name of the Lord. On the other hand, it is equally important that we ask ourselves how often we have taken the steps to actively prevent this from happening by choosing to make His name hallowed.

While true holiness can be difficult to comprehend, another perspective on it can help us come closer to that understanding. *Vine's Expository Dictionary of the New Testament* identifies the Greek word for "hallowed" to be connected with the idea of holiness and defines it by associating it with its Greek opposite: "common."[17] In other words, the concept of "hallowed be Your name" could be understood to mean: prevent Your name from becoming common.

Jesus wasn't merely suggesting that we give praises to the Lord at the beginning of our prayers, but rather that we become a people through whom

God's glory could be revealed to the earth. We might also open the Lord's Prayer with these words: "Our Father in heaven, make Your name extraordinary and glorify it in the earth."

> *Now to him who is able to do far more abundantly than all that we ask or think, according to the power at work within us, to him be glory in the church and in Christ Jesus throughout all generations, forever and ever. Amen.*
>
> Ephesians 3:20–21 ESV

Cyprian, the bishop of Carthage, writing in the third century, suggested that it was not reasonable to assume that God's name might be made holy by our prayers.[18] If this is true, then why would Jesus instruct us to pray in such a fashion? Wouldn't it be more likely that this phrase is just an expression of praise and nothing more? If it is not through our prayers that God's name is glorified or hallowed and this phrase is not solely an expression of praise and worship, then what is it that we are asking God for?

> *So I will show my greatness and my holiness and make myself known in the eyes of many nations. Then they will know that I am the Lord.*
>
> Ezekiel 38:23 ESV

The emphasis of this passage is upon the fact that God will reveal His greatness and His holiness, rather than on the idea that we can make Him more holy by our praise and worship. Perhaps, then, our petition has more to do with asking God to make Himself known in us and through us, so that we can be a part of revealing Him in the earth.

In the late fourth and early fifth century, the patriarch of Alexandria, Cyril, acknowledged this idea, that we cannot make God more holy as we pray, for He is the holiest of all things holy. He went on to write:

> *If a person says, "Our Father, hallowed be your name," he is not requesting any addition be made to God's holiness. He rather asks that he may possess such a mind and faith to feel that His name is honorable and holy.*[19]

So, how does God make His name holy in the earth? He does it through His people. By making His people holy, He reveals His own holiness to those in the earth around them. This idea is supported by the words of Ephesians 3, where we are reminded that part of the way He is glorified is "according to the power that works in us" (v. 20 NKJV), and Ezekiel's acknowledgment (Ezekiel 38:23) that His holiness will be visibly seen in the eyes of many nations.

Wow! Could Jesus actually be suggesting that we can have an integral part in helping the world see the holiness of our Father? When we consider this instruction on prayer in connection with the admonition that we should "be holy in all [our] conduct, because it is written, 'Be holy, for I am holy,'"[20] this would certainly seem to be the case.

Is it possible that in addition to an expression of worship as we open our prayer to our Father, this is also a petition that He make Himself known to all the earth both in us and through us? Is such a prayer so far-fetched? Consider the words of Jesus only a few verses later:

> *You are the light of the world. A city set on a hill cannot be hidden. Nor do people light a lamp and put it under a basket, but on a stand, and it gives light to all in the house. In the same way, let your light shine before others, so that they may see your good works and give glory to your Father who is in heaven.*
>
> Matthew 5:14–16 ESV

Jesus actually goes on to direct us to let our light shine so that men can see our good works and give glory to and acknowledge the holiness of our Father. Now the question becomes, just how do we go about allowing His holiness to be seen in us?

Your Name

Notice that Jesus did not simply suggest that we pray for God to show the world His holiness through us, but that He might make His name holy through us. This is a prayer that His name be made manifest in us. Throughout scripture we find that names are more significant than our current culture would lead us to believe. A name is so important in scripture that God sometimes changed the name of a person to reflect a change in their character or nature. Abram ("exalted father") became Abraham ("father of a multitude"); Jacob ("supplanter") became Israel ("God prevails"); and Saul ("demanded") became Paul ("humble").

Is it any wonder that our Father cannot be identified by a single name, even though that was something people desperately wanted to know? Moses asked God for His name so that he could identify Him to the people. God responded by declaring, "I AM who I AM."[21] As scripture unfolds, God reveals many aspects of His character and nature as He reveals more names by which He can be known. Consider just a few:

Jehovah-Jireh:	The Lord will provide
Jehovah-Nissi:	The Lord my banner (He goes before as a protector)
Jehovah-Shalom:	The Lord is peace
Jehovah-Shammah:	The Lord is there (His presence is with us)
Jehovah-Tsebaoth:	The Lord of hosts (He is powerful)
Jehovah-Tsid-Kenu:	The Lord our righteousness
Jehovah-Raah:	The Lord our shepherd
Jehovah-Rapha:	The Lord our healer

And the list could go on and on. Do you truly know the God whom you serve? Do you know His name? If you do, He is exactly the Who and the What that you need right now.

The names of God are amazing, but what do they have to do with praying for Him to make us holy or to make His holiness known through us? To answer that, the next question might be, do I know who I am? All of creation is waiting for us to recognize who we are.

> *For the creation waits with eager longing for the revealing of the sons of God. For the creation was subjected to futility, not willingly, but because of him who subjected it, in hope that the creation itself will be set free from its bondage to decay and obtain the freedom of the glory of the children of God. For we know that the whole creation has been groaning together in the pains of childbirth until now.*
>
> Romans 8:19–22 ESV

If we are Christians, then we are sons of God—for we are all sons of God through faith in Christ Jesus.[22] Creation is waiting for us to recognize that we are sons of God—His children—and when we know who we are, when we become holy as He is holy, then creation will be delivered from the bondage that the Fall of man subjected it to.

If we are sons of God, then we bear His name. Think about it. This is the one thing that every male child carries forward for the generations to come—the name of his father. As sons (both male and female can be the "sons" identified by scripture) of God, we carry the name of our Father. When Jesus taught us to pray "hallowed be Your name," He was teaching us to pray that the names of God might be made manifest in us and that His name would then be made holy in the earth through us.

You are a healer, a provider, a protector. You are not just John/Jane Doe, you are John Rapha, Jane Jireh, John/Jane Nissi. You are a present help in time of need and the peace of God manifest in the earth. When you do not display these qualities, then His name is at risk of being profaned, and when you do display these qualities, then His name is made extraordinary and uncommonly good in the earth.

According to 2 Corinthians 6:16, "you are the temple of the living God." Haggai 2:9 suggests that the former temple (one created of wood and stones) is less glorious than the latter temple (one made of flesh and blood). But do you know why the temple was built in the first place? Solomon explains why it was in the heart of his father, David, to build the temple and what has been completed by his building of it.

> *Then the king turned around and blessed all the assembly of Israel, while all the assembly of Israel stood. And he said, "Blessed be the Lord, the God of Israel, who with his hand has fulfilled what he promised with his mouth to David my father, saying, 'Since the day that I brought my people Israel out of Egypt, I chose no city out of all the tribes of Israel in which to build a house, <u>that my name might be there</u>. But I chose David to be over my people Israel.'*

> *Now it was in the heart of David my father <u>to build a house for the name of the Lord</u>, the God of Israel. But the Lord said to David my father, 'Whereas it was in your heart to build <u>a house for my name</u>, you did well that it was in your heart. Nevertheless, you shall not build the house, but your son who shall be born to you shall build the <u>house for my name</u>.' Now the Lord has fulfilled his promise that he made. For I have risen in the place of David my father, and sit on the throne of Israel, as the Lord promised, and <u>I have built the house for the name of the Lord</u>, the God of Israel."*
>
> 1 Kings 8:14–20 ESV (emphasis added)

The reason it was in the heart of both David and Solomon to build a temple was because God put within them the desire to build a place to house the name of God. If, as Haggai suggests, the temple of flesh displays more glory than the temple of wood and stone, then by carrying His name you display His glory and make His holiness known.

Psalm 138:2 declares that His Word has been magnified above His name. We, of course, know that the Word of God is made manifest in His Son, Jesus.[23] So, when we invite Jesus, the Word of God, into our hearts, we become the latter temple—the temple of the living Word of God. Now consider one of the most significant things that Jesus did while upon the earth:

I have manifested your name to the people whom you gave me out of the world. Yours they were, and you gave them to me, and they have kept your word.
John 17:6 ESV (emphasis added)

One of Jesus' primary purposes was to make visible or make known the name of God that had been hidden or unknown. Both His words and His deeds restored holiness to the name of God in the earth. You, as a son of God, bear His name. You, as the temple of God, carry His name. You, doing the things Jesus did,[24] manifest His name.

"Hallowed be Your name." Our Father in heaven—make Your name holy! Reveal Yourself through us. Help us not only to avoid profaning Your name, but also to demonstrate the fact that You are extraordinary and that there is none like You. Allow us to carry Your name in such a way that others see You reflected and revealed in our lives.

Breaking Bread

Hallowed Be Your Name
(Matthew 6:9)

EXAMINE

Has "our Father's" name become commonplace in the earth today? If so, what can you do to help make it extraordinary again?

_____

_____

_____

_____

What can you do to help prevent God's name from being profaned by our contemporary culture? (See Leviticus 22:31–33.)

_____

_____

_____

_____

Is there any particular area of your life where you need the Lord to restore and refresh in order that you might become a more fitting habitation for His name? If so, what is it and what is it in need of?

_____

_____

_____

_____

If changing your last name so that you were literally identified by one of God's names would instantly allow you to walk in that aspect of His character, which name would you choose? Why?

_____

_____

_____

_____

REFLECT

Take some time this week to reflect on the phrase "hallowed be Your name" from Matthew 6:9. Reflect on what it means to be a part of the manifestation of

God's holiness in the earth. Set aside at least fifteen minutes to spend just being quiet and listening.

ACT

Write down five things that you can do this week to either help make the extraordinary nature of who God is better known, or to help prevent His name from being profaned. Actively endeavor to accomplish at least two of the things you listed within the next seven days. At the end of one week, write a short testimony of how you completed this assignment.

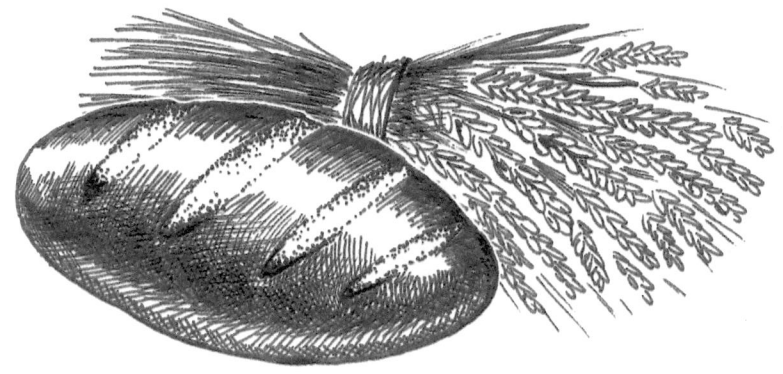

Chapter 4
Your Kingdom Come

The Kingdom of God is a broad and amazing subject. In fact, a book could easily be written on this subject alone. In the context of the Lord's Prayer, Jesus instructed His disciples that, as a part of their prayer lives, it was important to pray that God's Kingdom come. While it is important to consider, at least on a basic level, what the Kingdom of God really is, our starting point for examining this aspect of the model prayer is to determine why it needs to come. Somehow we often assume that Jesus was giving us an instruction to pray that the Kingdom of God would begin. If this is not the intention of this phrase in the prayer, then what is? As we have already clearly seen, there is often much more involved in the instructions Jesus was giving than can first be identified from the words alone. This is one of those times when even the words in Greek, from which this phrase is translated, do not fully give us an understanding of what Jesus was saying to His disciples.

When Does the Kingdom Begin?

The Greek word translated "come" is *erchomai* (er'-khom-ahee), and it can properly be translated as "to come into being" or "to make its appearance." God no more needs us to pray for His Kingdom to come into existence than He does for us to pray that His holiness be increased in some fashion. On the other hand, the second possible translation provides at least a bit more insight. While we may not need to pray for God's Kingdom to come into being, it does feel right to pray that it be revealed or make its appearance. By looking at the Hebrew culture of Jesus, we can gain more insight than the literal words could provide for us alone.

In the Hebrew culture, there would have been no concept of a coming kingdom (at least not in the way we think of it when we examine this prayer). Rather, there would have been a mind-set that reflected the words of the Kaddish, a prayer hymn that is central to a Jewish prayer service. Just as in the opening of the Lord's Prayer, the central focus of the Kiddish is on magnifying the name of God. One of its lines essentially declares: "May He cause His Kingdom to reign." With this in mind (and a recognition that a final possible meaning of the Greek word translated as "come" could be "to come from one place to another"), this portion of the Lord's Prayer might more clearly be read as: "May You continue to establish Your Kingdom and make it known...."

The Kingdom of God is not something we hope to see one day in the distant future, but rather it is something that is already present. When we pray for the Kingdom to come, we are asking God to open our eyes that we might see and participate in what is already in existence around us—that we might become a part of expressing its presence in the earth.

The Kingdom itself holds a central place of prominence in the New Testament. John the Baptist's core message was one of the Kingdom:

> *In those days John the Baptist came preaching in the wilderness of Judea, "Repent, for the kingdom of heaven is at hand."*
>
> Matthew 3:1–2 ESV

When John was confined to prison, Jesus then took up His message of the Kingdom:

> *From that time Jesus began to preach, saying, "Repent, for the kingdom of heaven is at hand."*
>
> Matthew 4:17 ESV

Before Jesus was crucified and ascended into heaven, He instructed His disciples to continue to declare this message of the kingdom,[25] which they did.[26]

It is not for us to pray the Kingdom into existence, but rather that we might come to experience it in all its glory. This is exactly what the disciples would have understood when Jesus spoke and for the first few centuries that followed.

Augustine, bishop of Hippo, who was born in the mid-fourth century and was considered one of the greatest theologians of Western Christianity, put it this way:

> *Some might get the strange impression that "come" implies "for the first time upon the earth"—as if to imply that God were not even now really reigning upon the earth! Or God had not always reigned upon the earth from the foundation of the world!*[27]

As we ponder his words, try to understand the presence of the Kingdom by doing the following experiment: Stop reading for a moment and close your eyes. When you do, keeping them closed, ask yourself if you really believe that there is no longer any light in the room.

—pause—

When you tried this experiment, isn't it more likely that light remained present in the room even when your eyes were closed, and that in reality, you just couldn't see it or couldn't see it fully? When you opened your eyes, were you really surprised that the light remained in the room, even though you couldn't see it when your eyes were closed? This is like the Kingdom of God. It's there whether you can see it or not.

We don't seek for the Kingdom to come in the sense of a beginning, but rather to come alive in our recognition. We pray for God to allow what has always been present to be made known or acknowledged in us. After all, whether we see it, feel it, or sense it in some way, does not change the fact that it is present. Augustine went on to describe this very idea:

> *Just as light that is present is absent to the blind or to those who shut their eyes, so the Kingdom of God though it never departs from the earth, yet is absent to those who know nothing about it.*[28]

That's exactly what Paul was describing when he said that the god of this world had blinded the minds of unbelievers and that they are prevented from seeing the light of the gospel.[29] The light is always present, but our eyes must be unveiled in order to recognize that presence.

What and Where Is the Kingdom?

If the Kingdom of God is not some theoretical concept that begins sometime in the future, but rather already exists all around us and is waiting to be revealed, then our prayer is really for God to allow us to live in it here and now. If we begin to believe that the Kingdom is ready to be revealed in this very moment, then we should also ask ourselves: What is it that we are asking to be revealed, and where will we find it?

Jesus was not teaching us to pray for an earthly kingdom to be established and become visible to the eye of the beholder. Nor was He suggesting a political system that would change the way the world perceived His instructions. The Kingdom of God is not a physical space, but rather something deeply spiritual. Paul wrote to the Romans that the Kingdom was not identified with earthly concepts like eating and drinking, but rather with spiritual concepts like peace and joy.[30] He further told the Corinthians that it was not made manifest by the spoken word, but rather in power.[31]

Simply put, when we ask the Father for His Kingdom to come, we are asking Him to make us more like Jesus. This is the reason we do not find the Kingdom by looking around us. Even if we understand what we are praying when we say, "Your Kingdom come," we are often found looking in the wrong places for it. People end up looking for the Kingdom just like the Pharisees, because they want to see something external that proves to them that God is real. Instead, we are called upon to accept Him by faith and expect that the Kingdom will then exist within us. This is the reason that praying for the Kingdom to come is about it being revealed in us and through us!

> *Now when He was asked by the Pharisees when the kingdom of God would come, He answered them and said, "The kingdom of*

God does not come with observation; nor will they say, 'See here!' or 'See there!' For indeed, the kingdom of God is within you."
Luke 17:20–21 NKJV

Whether you realize it or not, to pray the Lord's Prayer properly is to pray that the Kingdom of God, which already exists within us as believers, be revealed both to us and to the world around us, and the only way that can be done is for it to come through us. This portion of the prayer is an introduction to spiritual warfare, because it is a warfare prayer. If this prayer is to be answered by God, then it requires a battle to take place. Shortly after teaching the disciples this prayer, Jesus would explain to them that the Kingdom had been and was going to continue to require forceful advancement because the violence of the spiritual war that had begun would prevent its growth.[32]

To put it bluntly, if we are to see this prayer answered, then we can only gain the ability to live a Kingdom life when we win the battle within us—the battle between our soul (i.e., mind, will, emotions) and our spirit for who will rule. All of our intellect, learning, reasoning, worldly wisdom, effort, striving, and passion still leaves us coming up short. We are destitute when it comes to bringing the Kingdom into view.

While some might suggest that this is not the proper attitude for a Christian—that we should be bold and confident overcomers, people of faith, and possessors of a positive confession—they would be misunderstanding the difference between the internal battle and the external evidence. Matthew 5:3 makes it clear that the Kingdom of heaven belongs to the "poor in spirit." The phrase is the key to understanding that difference. The word *poor* is taken from a Greek word, *ptocheuo* (pto-khyoo'-o), which at its base level means to be a beggar. Prior to its popularization in the Gospels, it was never used in a positive sense. In short, the word conveyed the idea of being poor, weak, afflicted, and reduced to want and need. So, if Matthew is correct, when we pray for the Kingdom to come, we are asking for something that we have absolutely no ability to help bring to pass. To be able to reveal the Kingdom, we must realize that it must be freely given to us and that we are crying out for something we do not have, nor do we have the capability to create. When we pray "Your Kingdom come," He reveals it within us for all the world to see, and according to Isaiah 55:1–3, He allows us to "buy" it without money.

The Kingdom exists within us, and a battle is raging as to whether or not it will expand and be seen through us. In praying for the Kingdom to come, we are entering into warfare and asking God to allow something we could never have on our own, to not only exist inside of us, but to flow out of us. Matthew describes for us how the Kingdom flows through us as disciples of the King when he writes:

> *And proclaim as you go, saying, "The kingdom of heaven is at hand." Heal the sick, raise the dead, cleanse lepers, cast out demons. You received without paying; give without pay.*
>
> Matthew 10:7–8 ESV

How Do We Know the Kingdom Has Come?

The parables recorded in the book of Matthew (predominantly in chapter 13) provide some of the best guidance available on whether or not our prayer is being answered. According to Matthew 13:11, these parables were actually given by Jesus in order that we might know the mysteries of the Kingdom. So what do these parables tell us about how to recognize the Kingdom as it begins to be made known through us?

1. The Kingdom Is Not Without Tension

Though it may seem strange, as we begin to see the Kingdom of God manifest through us, one of the primary indications that it is becoming visible is found in the fact that there will be imitators and counterfeiters. Our adversary, the devil, is incapable of creating anything new on his own and thus his weaponry has always consisted of what he could counterfeit and corrupt. As he sees the Kingdom begin to manifest, it is almost a certainty that he will use his best tools to prevent it, and as a result, the false will always testify that something real is on the horizon.

When two polar-opposite demonstrations of power exist side by side, there will be tension. The tendency may be for us to withdraw in fear that we will be drawn into error by that which is not of God; however, the tension created between that which is real and that which is false is one of our surest indications that the true Kingdom is present. There can be no counterfeit unless there is something real to be imitated. As a result, the more we see the existence of our adversary's corrupted imitations, the more certain we should become that the Kingdom exists in a very present way.

This principle is illustrated by the parable of the wheat and the tares as recorded in Matthew 13:24–43. The Master sows good seeds in the field; that is, he sows the "sons of the kingdom" or those who will display to the world the Kingdom of God that is within them. However, the enemy comes and sows tares among the wheat; that is, he sows "sons of the wicked one." In other words, he sows seeds intended to corrupt the sons of the Kingdom and introduces counterfeit sons of his own. Both the wheat and the tares grow up together until a point in time comes when they can be distinguished easily and separated. Thus, the existence of the counterfeit is evidence that the real thing is present.

2. *The Kingdom Will Grow Within Us*
Another excellent indication that the Kingdom of God is beginning to grow within us is to ask ourselves, "Am I complacent or content?" Complacency can be defined as being unaware or uninformed of that which is around us and thus entering a deceptive state of self-satisfaction. Paul, on the other hand, indicated that in

whatever situation he found himself, he could be content.[33] Contentment conveys the idea of being happy and is used by Paul to describe the state of continuing to press forward with joy, no matter the current circumstances. The first suggests the idea of stagnation, while the second suggests the idea of ongoing growth. If the Kingdom is being manifest through us, then we should be content, but never complacent.

Contentment will without exception produce growth, while complacency will stifle it. Though a seed is buried beneath the surface of the ground and must actually die in order to spring forth in life and growth,[34] there is a recognition that it is doing what it was created for. Complacency results from a lack of knowledge, particularly knowledge of who we are and what we were created for, thus preventing growth and destroying us in the process.[35]

The parable of the mustard seed as found in Matthew 13:31-32 illustrates this principle. In this parable, the Kingdom of heaven is compared to a mustard seed that is sown in the field. The mustard seed is tiny in comparison to all the other seeds and miniscule in comparison to the field itself, yet it is not limited by its circumstances or situation. Instead, the mustard seed begins to grow and it continues to grow as long as it lives, becoming so large that it even becomes a place of refuge for other elements of God's creation.

3. The Kingdom Will Affect Every Part of Our Lives
Once we have experienced Kingdom-minded Christianity, we can never again be the same. When we pray for God's Kingdom to come and the battle within us begins, it will affect every aspect of our lives. The presence of the Kingdom of God, when awakened in us, will begin to permeate our entire beings and change the very core of who we are. When the Kingdom begins to spring forth and become visible, no part of our character can remain hidden in the dark, and instead, it will be exposed to the light and transformed into the image of the One who is light.[36]

This principle is described by the parable of the leaven as found in Matthew 13:33. Here Jesus compares the Kingdom to leaven and indicates that just as leaven works, when the Kingdom is released within us, it will work its way throughout us until every aspect of who we are is affected by it.

4. The Kingdom Will Cost Us Everything
While we may not have anything to offer in order to obtain the Kingdom, once it has been identified and released within us, it will cost us everything. The Kingdom requires that we trade our thoughts for His thoughts and our desires for His desires. The good news, as described by Psalm 37:4, is that when we place our delight in the Lord, He begins to assign His desires to us so they can begin to be made manifest through us. Although it may cost us everything, the Kingdom is worth it.

It is important that we keep in mind that though the Kingdom cost us everything, there is actually nothing we have that is of lasting value. The temporal things we hold dear may be lost, but they are exchanged for that which truly has everlasting value, and in giving it all up, we have more to gain than we do to lose.

Matthew 13:44-46 presents the parables of the treasure hidden in the field and the pearl of great price. These two parables illustrate the reward that results from giving up everything for the Kingdom. When we first see the Kingdom that is hidden within us, the value of having it manifest through us becomes apparent. In order for the Kingdom to be revealed through us as Jesus taught us to pray, we must trade in all that seemed to be of value in the world for what carries real value in the Spirit.

5. The Kingdom Will Change the World Around Us
Finally, it is important to remember that when the Kingdom of God begins to be revealed, it doesn't just change us, but it will have an impact upon everyone around us. As we express the Kingdom, creation around us must come into alignment with it. As Jesus explained in the parable of the wheat and tares, He was sowing the "sons of the kingdom." It is these very sons that creation is longing to be made manifest, so that it might be set free.[37] When the Kingdom begins to be revealed though us, there is an opportunity to give away what we freely received and that will change the people who received it.[38]

While there may not be a parable in Matthew 13 to illustrate this point, Matthew does make clear that this is what happened everywhere that Jesus, the perfect manifestation of the Kingdom of God, went.

> *And Jesus went throughout all the cities and villages, teaching in their synagogues and proclaiming the gospel of the kingdom and healing every disease and every affliction.*
> Matthew 9:35 ESV

> *But if it is by the Spirit of God that I cast out demons, then the kingdom of God has come upon you.*
> Matthew 12:28 ESV

When the Kingdom exists within us and begins to be revealed through us, as Jesus taught us to pray, then we will begin to do the things that Jesus did and even greater works,[39] and the world around us will, by necessity, be changed.

"Your Kingdom come." Make Your eternal Kingdom known throughout the earth. Use us to illustrate the majesty of Your Kingdom and let Your light so shine through us that all men are made aware of its presence. Push

back the counterfeit as You reveal Your truth and cause Your Kingdom to grow in us and through us in such a way that it reclaims all that the enemy has stolen.

Breaking Bread

Your Kingdom Come
(Matthew 6:10)

EXAMINE

Are the Kingdom of God and the Kingdom of heaven the same thing? Why or why not?

_____

_____

_____

_____

The Kingdom of God is within you (Luke 17:20–21), but it must also be taken by force (Matthew 11:12). What needs to occur in your life to see the Kingdom come?

_____

_____

_____

_____

How can we reconcile the fact that we must become "poor in spirit" in order to establish the Kingdom of heaven (Matthew 5:3), yet we are also to trust God to supply all of our needs (Philippians 4:19)?

_____

_____

_____

_____

If we have nothing of our own to offer in exchange for the Kingdom, then how can it cost us everything? Consider 1 John 2:15 and Romans 12:2 as you answer.

_____

_____

_____

_____

REFLECT

Take some time this week to reflect on the phrase "Your Kingdom come" from Matthew 6:10. Reflect on what areas of your life need to be conquered or submitted to the King in order to establish His

Kingdom. Set aside at least fifteen minutes to spend just being quiet and listening.

ACT

Write down at least five areas in your life that need to be submitted to the authority of the King. Choose one of these areas and offer it to the Lord as a "fast" this week. Specifically choose to abstain from the attitudes, actions, or thoughts that have occupied your heart in that area, and ask the Lord to fill the empty space that it creates with His presence, allowing that presence to establish His Kingdom within you.

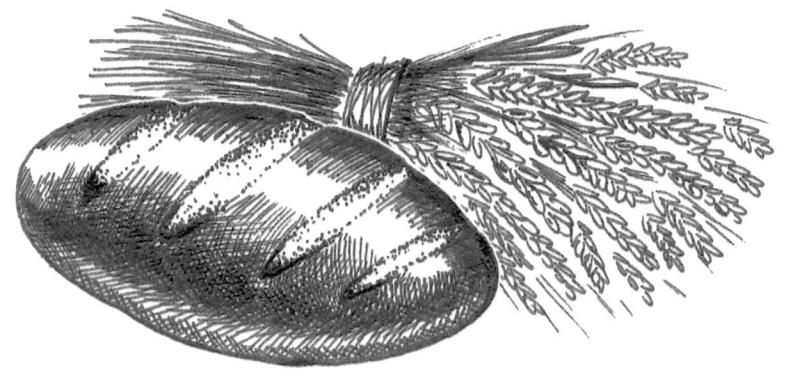

Chapter 5
Your Will Be Done

When it comes to acting by faith in our prayer life, it is essential that we know and understand the will of God when we pray. For this reason, it is not surprising that Jesus would include instructions that we pray for the will of His Father to be done.

These two phrases, concerning the Kingdom coming and God's will being done, are both distinct and interconnected. Before we consider the specifics associated with praying for the will of God to be done, take into account the significance of that connection: If we do not know (and do) the will of God, then we cannot enter the Kingdom of God. Jesus makes this connection clear with the instructions Matthew records in the very next chapter:

> *Not everyone who says to me, "Lord, Lord," will enter the kingdom of heaven, but the one who does the will of my Father who is in heaven.*
>
> Matthew 7:21 ESV

This connection between the Kingdom of God and the will of God cannot be overlooked. As we have already considered, Jesus was the perfect example of one who lived a life demonstrating the Kingdom of God. This connection is at the heart of what Jesus meant when He declared that He only did what He saw the Father doing[40] and that He did not speak of His own accord, but only what His Father commanded Him to speak.[41]

Knowing God's Will

Much like praying for the Kingdom to come, when we pray for God's will to be done, we are not praying in order to somehow help God accomplish His will in the earth—it WILL be done. Neither are we being instructed to pray with a reckless abandon, hoping that we will occasionally happen upon the will of God. Jesus' instruction that we should pray "Your will be done" presupposes that we would know the will of God. Unfortunately, we often hear people praying in direct contradiction to this presupposition. This misguided form of prayer generally takes the shape of language similar to, "Father, if it be Your will…" While it cannot be said that such a prayer is completely ineffective, it would certainly seem that it is less effective than knowing and praying the will of God. More importantly, such a prayer doesn't seem to be consistent with the pattern that Jesus established by the example He set forth in both prayer and action.

If you are like many Christians today, the response to this idea that we should know the will of God is to raise our defenses and retreat into a stronghold established on an expectation of impossibility. I trust that by the fact that you are reading these pages, you are indeed not like many Christians today and will not immediately make that jump. Jesus set the example of saying only what He heard and doing only what He saw. He went on to explain that He could do this because He knew the will of the Father, and that He knew the will of the Father because He sought it out.

> *I can do nothing on my own. As I hear, I judge, and my judgment is just, because I seek not my own will but the will of him who sent me.*
>
> John 5:30 ESV

Jesus Himself set the example that we can know the will of God and thus we can pray accordingly. In some ways, what Jesus was teaching us in the Lord's Prayer was that we should pray for the will of God to be done in much the same way that we pray for the Kingdom of God to come. We are to ask for the will of God to be made known in us and demonstrated through us. Lest we continue to fear that this is not possible, remember Paul's words to the Ephesians when he told them not to be unwise, but to understand what the will of the Lord is.[42] Not only did Paul indicate that it is possible to know and understand the will of God, he actively prayed for others to recognize it—that they be filled with the knowledge of His will in all wisdom and spiritual understanding.[43] If we can know God's will, then there is no longer any need to pray "...if it be Your will."

Learning to Listen

If we want to know the will of God, then we must first learn to hear the voice of God. Certainly His will is revealed to us in the words of Scripture, but there is a deeper revelation of His will available to us when we personally hear His voice. Keep in mind, however, that His personal word to us will never violate His public words recorded in the Bible, and all that we hear when we listen for His voice must be judged against His written Word. While we hold the Word of God infallible and the standard by which all else is judged, we must also never confuse every drop of ink on the page with the will of God itself. For example, we know that it is the will of God that none should perish,[44] yet within the written Word of God, we find stories concerning some who have perished. From this we know that everything written in the Bible is the Word of God, but not every word in the Bible is the will of God. Learning to listen to God's voice is essential to knowing and understanding His will.

We must remember that just praying the sinner's prayer does not mean that we automatically have ears that actually hear. Our ears must be trained to listen for the voice of our Father so that we, like Jesus, can know and follow what He is doing. People often assume that since they are Christians, they will hear God if He speaks to them. Some even plead for God to speak audibly, thinking that He isn't speaking at all if they can't hear Him. Unfortunately, the account recorded in the book of John describing an occasion when God did speak audibly paints a different picture.

> *"Father, glorify your name." Then a voice came from heaven: "I have glorified it, and I will glorify it again." The crowd that stood there and heard it said that it had thundered. Others said, "An angel has spoken to him." Jesus answered, "This voice has come for your sake, not mine."*
>
> John 12:28–30 ESV

In this passage we find God speaking audibly and Jesus hears every word that His Father says. Why? Because of a deep, abiding relationship with His Father and the fact that He had spent enough time with Him to know His voice.[45] On the other hand, not everyone present heard the words of the Father, despite the fact that He was speaking out loud in an audible voice for all to hear. Notice that the Father was not speaking for Jesus to hear the words (Jesus already knew what the Father had to say), but rather for the people's sake (v. 30), yet some heard thunder, some heard what they misperceived to be an angel, and apparently, some heard nothing at all (v. 29).

To understand this concept requires us to both value the written Word of God and to draw near enough to our Father that we don't miss His instruction when He speaks. We must become aware that reading the Bible is both our standard and our starting point for knowing the will of God. It will provide us with the baseline against which all other matters may be judged, but reading it is not the complete process by which we discern His specific will for our lives and our prayer life. The psalmist hinted at what it takes to live a life directed by the will of God when he wrote:

> *Delight yourself in the Lord, and he will give you the desires of your heart.*
>
> Psalm 37:4 ESV

This passage suggests that relationship (time spent with the Father) is vital to receiving an understanding of His will. The Hebrew word translated as "give" here actually means "to assign." When we spend time delighting in fellowship with the Father, He will assign us His desires, or, in other words, He will instill His will in our hearts so that we can be participants in doing it. One of the things we are asking when we pray, "Your will be done," is that we might have increased fellowship with God, that we might delight ourselves in Him more and thus discern the will of God so that it may be done through us.

As we begin to spend time in fellowship with our Father and delight in Him, we are softened and become more pliable. In fact, this is the very thing that the Hebrew word used for "delight" means. In effect, we become the clay on the potter's wheel being shaped and molded by the will of the potter.[46] Having a listening ear is essential to this process, and as we begin to use our spiritual ears to hear, the Word of God promises we will shine forth as the sun in the Kingdom of our Father.[47]

Learning to Do

While learning to hear God's voice is absolutely possible and certainly a necessary component to the prayer that God's will be done, it is not the primary lesson Jesus was teaching us through this phrase. Jesus' instruction to pray, "Your will be done," is actually less about discerning the will of God (remember, it is presupposed that we know that) and more about accomplishing the will of God. Since God's will is going to be accomplished in the broad sense, no matter what we do or what we think (He is sovereign, after all), it is perhaps more accurate to understand this phrase as "Your will be done in me and through me." In other words, we are actually asking God to allow us to be a participant in what He is doing in the earth.

The words recorded by John help us to understand that knowing the will of God is insufficient unless we are willing to act upon that knowledge.

> *Behold, I stand at the door and knock. If anyone hears my voice and opens the door, I will come in to him and eat with him, and he with me.*

Fresh Bread by Michael B. French

Revelation 3:20 ESV

Notice how it is not enough to simply hear the voice of God as He stands at the door of our heart and knocks, but rather it is necessary to both hear His voice and then take action on what has been heard by opening the door. To do otherwise is simply to offer lip service to God and does not truly honor Him,[48] making us hypocrites.

The writer of Hebrews prays that the Lord would make them complete so that they could do the will of God,[49] and the psalmist calls it a delight to do the will of God that is in his heart.[50] To pray this portion of the Lord's Prayer is to pray that God would allow us to become instruments of His will, and by necessity, this means we must be changed. It is our nature to pursue our own will, and we must overcome this obstacle if we are to see this prayer for God's will to be done answered in our own lives. Even Jesus faced this battle as He prayed in the Garden of Gethsemane:

> *And he said, "Abba, Father, all things are possible for you. Remove this cup from me. Yet not what I will, but what you will."*
>
> Mark 14:36 ESV

Jesus operated in the earth as fully man, and He dealt with the same personal issues that we deal with. Jesus' desire as a man was that He not have to die, yet He won the battle and submitted His own will to the will of the Father.

There is an old rabbinical saying that goes something like this: "Do His will as if it were your will." This is the heart of what Jesus taught us to pray when He said, "Your will be done." Just as Paul would later write to the Romans, Jesus was teaching us to pray that we might "be…transformed by the renewing of [our] mind, that [we] may prove what is that good, and acceptable, and perfect will of God."[51]

"Your will be done." Father, reveal Yourself to us in such a way that we no longer strive to simply know Your will, but that Your will is made known as we act upon it. Teach us to both hear and to obey. Draw us into an ever-deeper and more intimate relationship with You so that we may know Your voice and make it known.

Fresh Bread by Michael B. French

Breaking Bread

Your Will Be Done
(Matthew 6:10)

EXAMINE

How do you know when you are doing the will of God? Consider Matthew 7:21–22 as you answer.

_____

_____

_____

_____

What are some of the ways that you can actively submit your own will to the will of God?

_____

_____

_____

_____

John 10:27 says that God's sheep hear His voice and follow Him. How do you hear God's voice, and how do you know that it is His?

_____

_____

_____

_____

What does it mean to "delight yourself in the Lord" (Psalm 37:4 ESV)? It may be helpful to examine the Hebrew word *anag* (aw-nag'), Strong's number OT:6026, in answering this question.

_____

_____

_____

_____

How does your personal will affect the implementation of God's will in and through your life?

_____

_____

REFLECT

Take some time this week to reflect on the phrase "Your will be done" from Matthew 6:10. Reflect on how you hear God speak to you, as well as how clearly you understand Him when He does. Consider the impact this has on your ability to see the will of God done in and through your life. Set aside at least fifteen minutes to spend just being quiet and listening.

ACT

Practice listening to the voice of the Holy Spirit this week. Write down five things that you believe God spoke to you, and connect with a prayer partner to discuss the implications of what He said and how it can be applied in your everyday life. Take at least one positive, identifiable, and quantifiable step toward pursuing that area of God's will, and write a short testimony explaining the step you took.

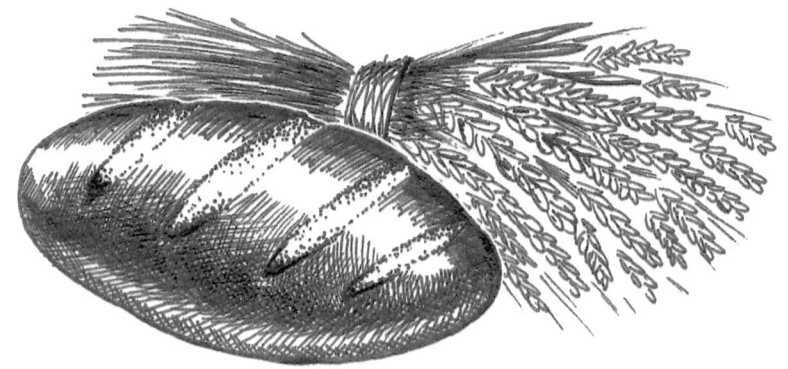

Chapter 6
On Earth As It Is in Heaven

Proverbs 25:2 (ESV) specifically declares that, "It is the glory of God to conceal things, but the glory of kings is to search things out." We are kings and priests[52] and it is our glory to search out the things of God. This next phrase from the Lord's Prayer helps us to know where to begin our search.

Heaven is not somewhere out beyond the stars; neither is it something that only exists for us in the distant future. When Jesus asked us to pray, "Your kingdom come, Your will be done, on earth as it is in heaven," He was reminding us that heaven is right here and right now and that this is both the where and the when of its existence. Yet more remains to uncover in the words of this phrase. The questions raised by this language in the Lord's Prayer are not limited to where and when heaven is, but they also create an interesting discussion on what heaven is.

What Is Heaven?

For many people, heaven has been relegated to a place filled with puffy white clouds where angels sit all day and strum their harps as they sing. Of course the more atheistic view of what heaven is limits it to the vast emptiness of space. In fact, when Yuri Gagarin became the first human to return to earth from a journey into outer space, Nikita Kruschev (the leader of the Soviet Union at that time) is said to have declared, "Gagarin flew into space, but didn't see any god there."[53] This mind-set held by atheists throughout history and carried into the modern era by Kruschev illustrates not only a lack of understanding about where heaven is, but a complete misperception about what heaven actually is. The very idea that someone could simply look around and see God resting on His sofa like one of the ancient Greek imposters is so contrary to the biblical image of both God and heaven that it is laughable.

While the Hebrew word often translated as "heaven" can be interpreted loosely enough to include the sky, it is more appropriately defined as "the abode of God." While the biblical view of God has Him neither seated upon a cloud nor lounging upon a sofa, it does indicate that He has a home, or an abode. Since there is no place where God is not, then heaven—His abode—must exist all around us and even within us. It is, in effect, a separate dimension that exists parallel with the natural world in which we interact. Such a dimension is frequently confused with the Eastern concept of Nirvana, or a place of profound peace of mind. We cannot allow this corrupted view of heaven that is expressed by false religious voices cause us to reject the biblical view of heaven.

To help separate the Eastern mind-set from the biblical view of heaven, we must recognize that while heaven is a separate dimension, it has not always been a place of peace as envisioned by those Eastern cultures. Lucifer once set himself against the Almighty in an attempted coup d'état, and that battle resulted in one-third of the heavenly hosts being cast out.[54] This war in heaven also helps us to understand a little more about what heaven is. Colossians 1:15–16 explains that God created everything both in heaven and on earth, both visible and invisible, and including thrones, dominions, principalities, and powers. From this, we understand that this separate dimension of heaven has many similarities with the world we live in. When this description from Colossians is coupled with Ephesians 6:12, which describes principalities, powers, rulers, and hosts, we begin to gain the insight that there is also a structure and order to heaven. Though it is a separate dimension existing parallel to our physical world, it is very real.

What Is Earth?

The Hebrew word translated as "earth" in Matthew 6:10 literally means "soil," and by extension, the whole globe, including its occupants. Earth then refers to the visible aspects of what Paul describes in Colossians 1, and because it is visible, it is much easier for us to comprehend. The parallels established in Colossians and Ephesians allow us to transpose some of our understanding of the things we see, to help us better understand what we do not see.

While the seat of God's authority, or His throne, may be in heaven, He has chosen to rest His feet upon and interact with the earth.[55] Prior to the Fall of mankind, there was little if any separation between these two dimensions of heaven and earth. God would step into the earth and walk with man in the cool of the evening for a time of consistent fellowship,[56] and that interaction was apparently a routine part of creation. It would seem that the portion of the earth we call the Garden of Eden, though on the earth, was to some degree or another virtually indistinguishable from heaven. At the Fall of man, a veil of separation was established, as embodied by the cherubim with their flaming swords who were put in place to guard the Tree of Life.[57]

It is important that we acknowledge a distinction between heaven and earth. The words used in this passage, even when they are as simple as "in" versus "on," are significant. The word translated as "in," as it relates to heaven, leaves us with the implication that it is something we are a part of. The original language can actually relate to the suggestion that we can be a part of heaven just like the contents of a book. On the other hand, when it comes to the earth, the word used is "on." Here the word suggests more of a place where we spend time temporarily. The original language translated "on" suggests simply being on the surface of something and not a part of it. We must recognize that as children of God, we are a part of the story of heaven, but we only have a temporary connection to this home we call earth.

Understanding what earth is seems far simpler than understanding what heaven is, but the journey to understand what Jesus was teaching us does not end there. The language Jesus used suggested that our prayers could reduce the intensity of the veil of separation that resulted from man's Fall. This then raises the question of how?

From Heaven to Earth
Psalm 67:1–2 suggests that God's will and His ways can be made known on the earth. It is possible that Jesus was referring to this psalm when He said, "Your kingdom come, your will be done, on earth as it is in heaven." Remember that the Kingdom of God is within us and the will of God is to be done through us. If His Kingdom exists within us, and His will is done through us, then the place it is to be done is *on* earth. Jesus was teaching us to ask God to establish a relationship with us and reveal Himself to us in such a way that

He might be made known *on* the earth just as He is known *in* heaven.

In fact, the very reason that Jesus was made incarnate, died, and rose again was to remove the veil that Adam's failure caused to be erected between heaven and earth (see Romans 5:12–21). When the veil was torn in the temple at the death of Jesus,[58] it was symbolic of the spiritual veil that had both separated man from God and earth from heaven. Jesus, who taught us to pray for the Kingdom and the will of God to be made known in earth as clearly as it was known in heaven, is also the very One who made it possible.

Scripture is filled with both direct and indirect references to a new heaven and a new earth. These references also seem to indicate that there will be little if any separation between these two dimensions when that time comes. If Jesus already "tore the veil," why then do we continue to experience this distinction and why was it necessary for Jesus to teach us to pray for it to cease being a hindrance to us? This is because the same adversary who used deception to entice Adam and Eve to eat of the fruit of the Tree of the Knowledge of Good and Evil, is continuing to use his craftiness to deceive us into a continued belief that the veil remains. Our enemy's entire goal is to wage war *on* the earth just as he did *in* heaven so that God's will might be thwarted and His Kingdom uprooted *on* earth though he was unable to accomplish it *in* heaven. Jesus taught us to pray for the strength to overcome this deception and become the instruments God uses to establish both His Kingdom and His will *on* earth until such time that the new heaven and earth are inseparable.

Throughout Jesus' teaching, He consistently made reference to this relationship between heaven and earth. We are not to lay up treasure *on* earth, but rather lay it up *in* heaven.[59] We are instructed that whatever we bind *on* earth will be bound *in* heaven and whatever we loose *on* earth will be loosed *in* heaven.[60] If we agree *on* earth concerning anything, it will be done by our Father *in* heaven.[61] Jesus also told His disciples that all authority had been given to Him *in* heaven and *on* earth before sending them out to make disciples themselves.[62] Finally, at the name of Jesus every knee will bow and every tongue will confess whether *in* heaven or *on* earth. Our lives are intended to tell the story of heaven during our temporary stay on earth.

Until that moment when heaven and earth are again as tangibly inseparable as they existed in Eden, there will be conflict; therefore, our understanding of this aspect of the Lord's Prayer remains crucial. Man was given dominion over the earth in the Garden, and that dominion was returned to him by the work Jesus did at Calvary. So long as man continues to walk in deceit, the earth will remain in bondage, just as Paul described it in Romans 8:18–25. But if we understand what Jesus was teaching us to pray, we can take on our true nature as the sons of God and be a part of bringing freedom from heaven into earth. Our prayer includes a petition for the will of God to be done in the earth to such a degree that creation is "loosed" from its bondage of corruption and takes on all the characteristics of the liberty of heaven. Before that moment in time arrives in its fullness, however, we pray as we were taught to pray, that we might see the Kingdom of heaven invade the earth as the will of God is done in us and through us.

"On earth as it is in heaven." We want to know You, Lord. To know You, not as some distant being who may occasionally interact with Your creation, but as a Father who lovingly and consistently reveals Yourself in and through Your creation. Respond to the groaning of creation and cause heaven to invade the earth at this very moment.

Breaking Bread

On Earth As It Is in Heaven
(Matthew 6:10)

EXAMINE

How does the understanding that heaven is not a place that can be physically discerned with our natural senses change the way you understand where God dwells?

_____

_____

_____

_____

Consider Colossians 1:15–16. What is the relationship between the following phrases: "heaven and earth," "visible and invisible," and "through him and for him"? How does this affect your understanding of this aspect of the Lord's Prayer?

_____

_____

A spiritual veil separates heaven from earth. Is it possible to pull back that veil and both see heaven and reveal it on the earth? If so, how?

How can your life be a part of revealing heaven on the earth?

REFLECT

Take some time this week to reflect on the phrase "on earth as it is in heaven" from Matthew 6:10. Reflect on how your life was created in order to tell the story of heaven on the earth. Set aside at least fifteen minutes to spend just being quiet and listening.

ACT

A preposition precedes a noun to show the noun's relationship to another word in the sentence. The preposition "on" precedes the noun "earth" to show the relationship between the earth and the Kingdom. The preposition "in" precedes the noun "heaven" to show the relationship between heaven and the Kingdom. With this in mind, what is the difference between "on" and "in"? Look up the definition of these two prepositions, and write a paragraph that explains how this changes your understanding of where heaven is.

Fresh Bread by Michael B. French

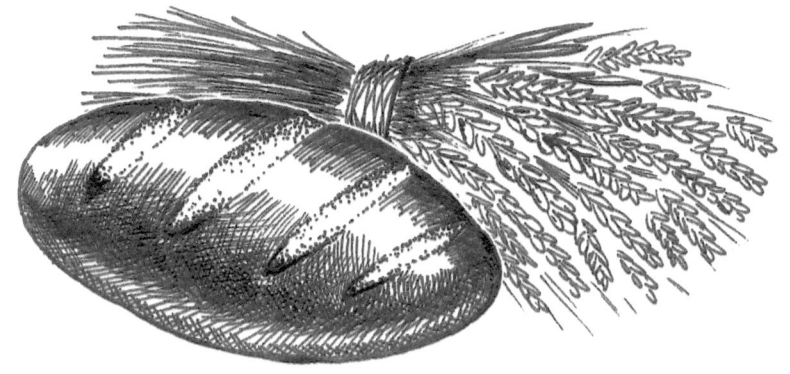

Chapter 7
Give Us This Day Our Daily Bread

In some ways the phrase, "give us this day our daily bread," is the most misunderstood portion of the Lord's Prayer. Even scholars agree that the meaning of this phrase is difficult to discern due to the presence of a single word—the word translated here as "daily." To understand why this passage is so challenging, and equally why it is so important, we must dig deeper than the English word and consider the Greek word *epiousios* (ep-ee-oo-sah). Interestingly, this passage and its parallel passage in Luke are the only two places where *epiousios* is used in the New Testament.

Even more interesting, these two uses of the word in the New Testament are virtually the only two places this Greek word is used in any recorded document of any kind.

Because of the rarity of this word, there is some dispute among scholars as to how it should be translated into English, and this makes understanding what Jesus was teaching by the use of this phrase a bit more challenging. Most, if not all, English translations of this passage use the phrase "daily bread"; however, the Latin translation of the New Testament would be more akin to the phrase, "Give us this day the bread needed for our sustenance." In either case, Jesus was discussing something deeper than merely a prayer of thanksgiving for our food.

That Which We Need

Too often, we have read Matthew 6:11 as though it were the following prayer children would pray before a meal:

> *God is great, God is good,*
> *Let us thank Him for our food,*
> *By His hand we are fed,*
> *Thank You, Lord, for our daily bread.*

This children's prayer is oft-repeated, but seldom prayed from the heart, and the same frequently holds true of the Lord's Prayer. When not seen as a memorized prayer of thanksgiving for the food that we are about to eat, others have suggested this phrase is

Fresh Bread by Michael B. French

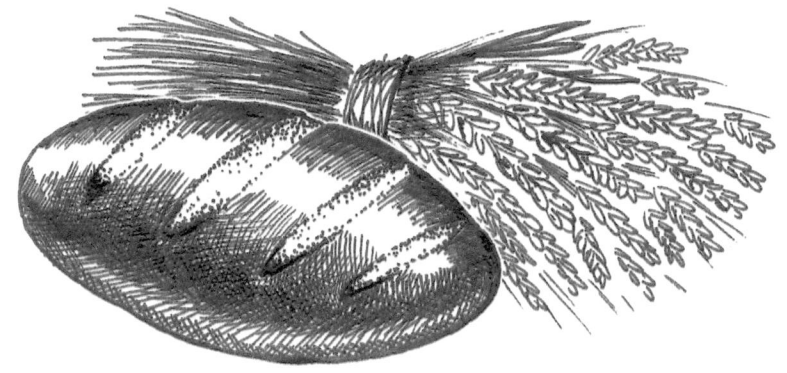

Chapter 7
Give Us This Day Our Daily Bread

In some ways the phrase, "give us this day our daily bread," is the most misunderstood portion of the Lord's Prayer. Even scholars agree that the meaning of this phrase is difficult to discern due to the presence of a single word—the word translated here as "daily." To understand why this passage is so challenging, and equally why it is so important, we must dig deeper than the English word and consider the Greek word *epiousios* (ep-ee-oo-sah). Interestingly, this passage and its parallel passage in Luke are the only two places where *epiousios* is used in the New Testament.

Even more interesting, these two uses of the word in the New Testament are virtually the only two places this Greek word is used in any recorded document of any kind.

Because of the rarity of this word, there is some dispute among scholars as to how it should be translated into English, and this makes understanding what Jesus was teaching by the use of this phrase a bit more challenging. Most, if not all, English translations of this passage use the phrase "daily bread"; however, the Latin translation of the New Testament would be more akin to the phrase, "Give us this day the bread needed for our sustenance." In either case, Jesus was discussing something deeper than merely a prayer of thanksgiving for our food.

That Which We Need
Too often, we have read Matthew 6:11 as though it were the following prayer children would pray before a meal:

> *God is great, God is good,*
> *Let us thank Him for our food,*
> *By His hand we are fed,*
> *Thank You, Lord, for our daily bread.*

This children's prayer is oft-repeated, but seldom prayed from the heart, and the same frequently holds true of the Lord's Prayer. When not seen as a memorized prayer of thanksgiving for the food that we are about to eat, others have suggested this phrase is a request for God to provide the food we will need to eat for tomorrow. In fact, this view of the phrase is actually more realistic, as it is supported by *Strong's Concordance* (which suggests the underlying language relates to "sufficient bread for tomorrow"), yet that understanding also seems too shallow for what has been drawn from the preceding phrases chosen by Jesus.

While asking God to provide what we need to eat in order to live another day seems very natural, it is in conflict with what Jesus taught only a few sentences later:

> *Therefore I tell you, do not be anxious about your life, what you will eat or what you will drink, nor about your body, what you will put on. Is not life more than food, and the body more than clothing? Look at the birds of the air: they neither sow nor reap nor gather into barns, and yet your heavenly Father feeds them. Are you not of more value than they? And which of you by being anxious can add a single hour to his span of life?*
> Matthew 6:25–27 ESV

Here Jesus is admonishing us not to worry about what we need to eat, but rather to trust that we are important to our Father and He will take care of us, just like He takes care of the birds of the air. Furthermore, Jesus would have been speaking from a

Jewish mind-set, and there is an old rabbinic question that addresses this topic as well:

> *In all the days of your life have you ever seen a wild animal or a bird laboring in a vocation? Yet, they are provided for without anxiety. They were created to serve me, but I was created to serve my Maker. How much more then should I be provided for without anxiety?*

For this to be merely a prayer of thanksgiving seems too shallow for the pattern already established, and to be a petition for the food we need to survive seems inconsistent with Jewish thought and the remainder of Jesus' message. What then is Jesus trying to teach us with these words?

A more consistent way of viewing this passage would be to understand that Jesus was teaching us to ask God to provide us with all we need in order to bring both the Kingdom of God and the will of God into a place of visibility on the earth through us. This was a prayer taught by a Master to His disciples. We should remember that a disciple is completely dependent upon his Master (in this case, God) for his every need. We were created to serve our Maker, and He will provide for us, physically and spiritually, without anxiety.

To understand this phrase even more, consider how often Jesus would reference Old Covenant scriptures (even when He did not directly quote them) and then reflect on the words of this passage:

> *Remove far from me falsehood and lying; give me neither poverty nor riches; feed me with the food that is needful for me, lest I be full and deny you and say, "Who is the Lord?" or lest I be poor and steal and profane the name of my God.*
> Proverbs 30:8–9 ESV

Jesus is teaching us that we need to seek God for just enough. Not too much, and not too little. Perhaps this phrase could be restated as, "Give me my daily portion, neither tremendous wealth, nor poverty, but rather what I need to fulfill Your plan."

The Bread of Life

If it is not simply natural food we are asking God to provide for us in this portion of the Lord's Prayer, then what is it we are requesting? The simple answer is that we are asking for just enough of Jesus in order that He might be clearly seen in us and through us. By requesting just enough, we are in no way limiting what God desires to do in us and through us, but rather we are asking for that which is needed or that which is necessary in order for us to fulfill our destiny. Still, this seems to contradict what is taught in many Christian circles—that we should constantly be asking God for more. More of His presence, more of His power, more of His wisdom.

Fresh Bread by Michael B. French

According to John 6:35, Jesus is the Bread of Life and those who come to Him will never hunger. Jesus described Himself here using the analogy of something that is eaten in order to sustain life. While that may be a difficult analogy for some, it is not by far the most challenging way He ever used it. Just a few verses later, He chooses an even more direct and controversial way to describe this same concept:

> *So Jesus said to them, "Truly, truly, I say to you, unless you eat the flesh of the Son of Man and drink his blood, you have no life in you. Whoever feeds on my flesh and drinks my blood has eternal life, and I will raise him up on the last day. For my flesh is true food, and my blood is true drink. Whoever feeds on my flesh and drinks my blood abides in me, and I in him. As the living Father sent me, and I live because of the Father, so whoever feeds on me, he also will live because of me."*
>
> John 6:53–57 ESV

This saying was so difficult to comprehend for those who heard it directly that many turned away and ceased to follow Jesus.[63] Since He would have obviously known how this teaching would be received, it must have been a significant enough truth to require it to be said, regardless of how it was received. Keep in mind that the previous day, Jesus had fed the five thousand with five loaves and two fish.[64] When they came searching for Him the following day, they were looking for another free meal. Jesus pressed them to understand that there was more to living a spiritual life than simply eating enough food to keep the body alive. He was inviting them to partake of Him—to taste and see that the Lord is good[65]—but most of them were too focused on the earthly world around them to understand. In their misunderstanding, they walked away from all that was offered to them. We, as they, have the opportunity to literally become partakers of the Lord Jesus Christ—to spiritually eat His flesh and drink His blood. Jesus taught us to pray for our daily bread, not because we are needful of physical sustenance, but because we are needful of His presence within us.

When we recognize that Jesus was not teaching us to pray for natural food (at the very least, that was not His primary instruction here) and that He would only a few breaths later tell us not to worry over what we would eat or drink naturally, then we can begin to accept that we should be asking the Father for the Bread of Life. When we understand the Lord's Prayer in this manner, it also brings greater clarity to a well-known, oft-quoted psalm.

> *I have been young, and now am old, yet I have not seen the righteous forsaken or his children begging for bread.*
>
> Psalm 37:25 ESV

Over the years, the question has been raised as to how this psalm can be true when we see poverty and lack all around us, even in the Christian community.

The answer becomes clear when we realize that the righteous understand that they are never lacking for the Bread of Life and all they need to do is ask God for their "daily bread."

Manna from Heaven

Of course, there will be those who argue that Jesus could not have intended that we ask for a daily portion of Him, because once we have partaken of the Bread of His Body, then we will never be hungry again. By this argument, as we have come to understand this portion of the Lord's Prayer, it would become unnecessary, since it is a petition for God to provide the bread that I need for today. While eating of the Bread of Life—Jesus—means that we will never hunger again, it does not mean that there is no need for us to partake of Him each day. In fact, even as Jesus described Himself as the Bread of Life, He implied that very idea of a daily refreshing that is indicated by the Lord's Prayer.

> *I am the bread of life. Your fathers ate the manna in the wilderness, and they died. This is the bread that comes down from heaven, so that one may eat of it and not die. I am the living bread that came down from heaven. If anyone eats of this bread, he will live forever. And the bread that I will give for the life of the world is my flesh.*
>
> John 6:48–51 ESV

In describing Himself as the Bread of Life, Jesus also compared Himself to the manna that was provided to the children of Israel in the wilderness. By this analogy, what is provided to us is enough for each day, and we must depend upon God to provide us with our daily portion. Exodus 16:4–6 describes the provision of manna as also being presented as a test. The people were to gather each day's portion as a test of whether or not they would walk in God's law. Only on the sixth day were they allowed to gather enough to see them through both that day and the next (the Sabbath). Verses 19–21 of the same chapter makes it clear that when they gathered more than the portion assigned for that day, it spoiled, bred worms, and stank.

Consider how the Lord tested them to see whether they would trust Him, by providing only enough to get through the day at hand as it relates to the Lord's Prayer. Partaking of the Bread of Life Himself means that we will never hunger again. Once we have tasted and seen that the Lord is good, we know where our provision is and can return to the Source day after day after day. We will never be forsaken, and we will never be forced to beg for bread. Each day we can pass the test as to whether or not we will walk in relationship to Jesus (or walk in His law, as it is described in Exodus 16).

Give us this day our daily bread! *Father, provide for us enough of You that we will be able to accomplish Your will and display Your Kingdom today. We have no need to worry about tomorrow, for it has enough worry of its own.* We are needful of Him today, and we should desire to be filled fresh by Him as each new day dawns.

> *The steadfast love of the Lord never ceases; his mercies never come to an end; they are new every morning; great is your faithfulness. "The Lord is my portion," says my soul, "therefore I will hope in him."*
> Lamentations 3:22-24 ESV

He is our portion, and our Father provides just what we need, new every morning. Jesus is that Food that is needful for us, just as was described in Proverbs 30:8-9. The food that is needful for us is what we should be seeking, and that is also why we need not seek for all of it at once, nor forsake it altogether. To have more than enough means the possibility of seeing ourselves as no longer needing Him in order to fulfill our destiny, yet to have none means we profane His name by believing we do not need Him in order to survive.

Perhaps it is an issue of semantics, but it is possible that we do not need more of God, and rather that we need more room to contain enough of Him to fulfill our purpose. At the end of his ministry, John the Baptist stated, "He must increase, but I must decrease."[66] In our eyes, there will always be someone who has more than we do—more anointing, greater gifting, stronger faith—and yet there is no one who can do what we have been called to do the way we can. If we change our mind-set from one of asking God for more, to asking God to increase our capacity, then the amount of manna we have permission to gather each day increases. In this way, His grace is always sufficient, and though we may see ourselves as weak, His power can be made perfect in us.[67] Whatever God has given you to do, He has promised He will always provide enough for you to do it. In this way, the parable of the talents from Matthew 25 can be fulfilled in our lives. If we are faithful in what we have the capacity to do today, then God will increase our capacity to carry more, because He then knows that we will be faithful over that increased capacity.

The words translated as "food that is needful to me" in Proverbs 30:8 are the Hebrew words *lechem chuki*, and the phrase could literally be translated as, "Feed me with the bread that You have appointed me to have." In other words, give us this day our daily bread, just enough of You that we would remain dependent, yet still be totally capable of displaying You to the world around us.

"Give us this day our daily bread." We need You, Jesus. Increase our capacity to be filled with You to the point that nothing is impossible, but that every circumstance we face and every situation we find ourselves in

bows to Your presence within us. Don't allow us to become prideful or arrogant as You fill us. Teach us that You are enough and that we never have to beg to be filled.

Breaking Bread

Give Us This Day Our Daily Bread
(Matthew 6:11)

EXAMINE

What is the difference between asking God for more and asking Him for a greater capacity to hold more of Him? Is this distinction important?

_____

_____

_____

_____

Is your prayer life more focused on asking God to meet your physical needs or on asking Him to be all that you need? How does your focus change your attitude toward prayer?

_____

_____

_____

Why do you think it is such a struggle to apply Matthew 6:25–27 to our lives and let go of anxiety over how we will be provided for in the future? Is this more difficult in our modern culture?

_____

_____

_____

_____

Lamentations 3:24 declares that the Lord is your portion. What is the most important aspect of His character that you need to be made manifest in your life today?

_____

_____

_____

_____

REFLECT

Take some time this week to reflect on the phrase "Give us this day our daily bread" from Matthew 6:11.

Reflect on what bread really is, as well as your capacity to "gather" it (as the Israelites gathered mana) each day. Set aside at least fifteen minutes to spend just being quiet and listening.

ACT

Practice listening to the voice of the Holy Spirit this week. Write down five attributes of God that you feel need to be reflected more in your life. Choose one of His attributes each day this week and focus on displaying it to the fullest extent possible in your life. Write down how focusing on being filled with that portion of His presence affected your day.

Fresh Bread by Michael B. French

Fresh Bread by Michael B. French

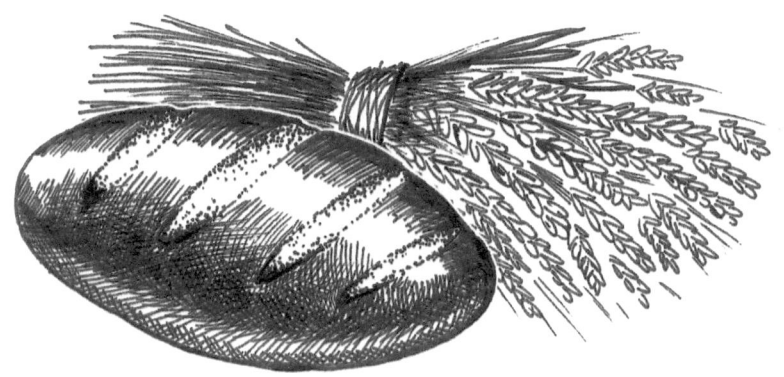

Chapter 8
Forgive Us Our Debts, As We Forgive Our Debtors

The beautiful language of the Lord's Prayer has been repeated by generations of believers (and non-believers alike) in multiple languages, and yet it continues to prove itself so much deeper than the surface understanding most individuals have of it. Nowhere is that more clear than when we consider the words of Matthew 6:12 and the powerful impact they can have on our lives if we truly believe them.

To put it simply, this portion of the prayer that Jesus used to teach us requires a tremendous price be paid if it is to be sincerely understood by those who pray it or use it to deepen their prayer life: Forgiveness must be given in order to be received.

The words that Jesus chose for this portion of the Lord's Prayer were intended to be crystal-clear. The comparison made here is in the form of a literary device known as a simile. A simile is a figure of speech that makes a comparison using the words *like* or *as* to show the similarities between two different things. Unlike a metaphor (often used in scripture), which implies a comparison, there is a direct comparison made when a simile is used. Matthew 6:11 solidified this direct comparison. Jesus and the prayer He was teaching us to pray are the equivalent of daily bread for our consumption. Here in verse 12 we are forgiven "as" we have forgiven—a direct comparison.

Forgive to Be Forgiven

Should there be any question as to what Jesus meant, He went on to clarify it in the two verses immediately following the prayer itself.

> *For if you forgive others their trespasses, your heavenly Father will also forgive you, but if you do not forgive others their trespasses, neither will your Father forgive your trespasses.*
>
> Matthew 6:14–15 ESV

Even if the words of the Lord's Prayer are unclear, could these words be made any clearer? If we cannot forgive those who have wronged us, then how can we expect to be pardoned by God for the wrongs we have committed? How can these words be misunderstood? Yet people seem to be either confusing or entirely ignoring that we attempt to obtain forgiveness without releasing others.

Matthew recounts this portion of the Lord's Prayer by using terms descriptive of a debt, while Luke uses the term *sin*.[68] There is little difference in the two versions, except that Luke is clarifying a specific meaning of the underlying phrase, while Matthew is making clear that forgiveness encompasses more than simply the idea of forgiveness of sin, by including any personal debt or moral obligation that might have an impact on our interpersonal relationships. The underlying Greek word *opheilema* relates to something owed or due, while the Hebrew term *chayav*, upon which some scholars feel the term in Matthew is drawn from, can mean both guilt for which one is held accountable and a debt to be paid.[69] Since we are examining the Lord's Prayer as recorded in Matthew, let us consider why Matthew chose to use language that broadens the understanding of what is being prayed.

Paul explained the impact of sin when he wrote his letter to the Romans.

> *For the wages of sin is death, but the free gift of God is eternal life in Christ Jesus our Lord.*
>
> Romans 6:23 ESV

When sin ruled in our lives, it paid us a wage and that wage is equated with death, according to Paul. If we are going to be free from sin, then the wages we receive must be repaid (which is what Jesus accomplished on our behalf through His death and resurrection), and our debt incurred from sin is cleared when we are forgiven. If we understand this principle, then it is not a stretch to recognize that those who sin against us are incurring a debt of death that we can forgive and, in fact, must forgive in order to receive the release from our own debt. When our eyes are opened to this truth, then we must also recognize the deeper truth Jesus meant when He said, "If [we] forgive the sins of anyone, they are forgiven; if [we] withhold forgiveness from anyone, it is withheld."[70]

Of course, the immediate rebuttal to this view of forgiveness is to ask, "Didn't Paul tell us that the gift of eternal life was free?"[71] The answer is most certainly—YES. However, our actions and attitudes can, and do, affect how we are able to receive it. Jesus explained this principle when He recounted the parable of the unforgiving servant.[72]

Simply put, the servant was freely given forgiveness of his enormous debt, yet his subsequent actions impacted his ability to receive and walk in that mercy. Don't misunderstand this concept as calling into question our salvation, but rather recognize that saved or not, when we refuse to forgive, we allow ourselves to be re-imprisoned for the debt we once carried, and it will impact our lives in substantially adverse ways. Refusing to forgive grants our adversary authority in our lives that can only be overcome by releasing forgiveness to those whom we have ourselves held captive.

When we consider the parable of the unforgiving servant and the impact his lack of forgiveness had on his life, the order that Jesus established in the language of this portion of the Lord's Prayer becomes extremely important. Jesus instructs that we must first forgive and then be forgiven. For a believer to receive true forgiveness from God, it can never be lost, because it would never have been received if we had not first forgiven. Matthew uses a verb tense (*Aorist*) that generally refers to an action that has either already taken place or is used to describe the individual steps in a continuous process with no division of the events. Thus, according to Matthew's account of this prayer, we must either forgive first or it must be an undivided part of the process of receiving our own forgiveness and of living our lives. Because God is timeless, the point in time when we forgive is not as significant as the ongoing process of imparting forgiveness.

The Importance of Relationship

With the significance of this portion of the Lord's Prayer now in focus, it is essential that we also understand why Matthew chose the broader term for *debt* instead of the more specific term for *sin*. As Matthew recounts the Lord's Prayer for the audience to which he writes, he is clearly indicating that our prayer should encompass the concept that our relationship with God is revealed through our relationships with others.

John makes this even clearer when he penned the following words from his first epistle.

> *If anyone says, "I love God," and hates his brother, he is a liar; for he who does not love his brother whom he has seen cannot love God whom he has not seen. And this commandment we have from him: whoever loves God must also love his brother.*
>
> 1 John 4:20–21 ESV

Perhaps this truth could also be expressed as, "If anyone says, 'I am forgiven,' and does not forgive his brother, he is a liar, for he who does not forgive his brother whom he has seen cannot be forgiven by God, whom he has not seen."

When we understand why Jesus taught us the way He did, we find deeper understanding in the words He used here in the Lord's Prayer. Jesus taught us to pray in such a way that we could know how close our relationship was to our Father. If we want to know how close we are to God, then we need only look at the relationships we have with those around us. For this to provide true and keen insight, we must also remember that looking at the worst of our natural relationships provides the deepest understanding of our relationship to God. This is the pattern God established when He forgave us while we were yet sinners[73] and when Jesus gave us the following instructions:

> *But I say to you, Love your enemies and pray for those who persecute you, so that you may be sons of your Father who is in heaven. For he makes his sun rise on the evil and on the good, and sends rain on the just and on the unjust. For if you love those who love you, what reward do you have? Do not even the tax collectors do the same? And if you greet only your brothers, what more are you doing than others? Do not even the Gentiles do the same? You therefore must be perfect, as your heavenly Father is perfect.*
>
> Matthew 5:44–48 ESV

The Challenges of Forgiveness

If we must forgive in order to be forgiven, the next questions that arise are: 1) Who needs our forgiveness? 2) When can we stop forgiving them? and 3) Will we ever forget what they did? Initially, the answer to these questions may appear to be simple, but when we dig a little deeper they may actually present some of our greatest challenges in walking out forgiveness.

When we consider whom we need to forgive, our first impression may be as simple as those who have offended us or sinned against us. However, to use this language alone may leave us in a position to omit some of those whom we need to release. Upon closer examination, Scripture seems to identify three classes of people who need to be forgiven in order for this prayer to be fulfilled.

The first group, and of course the most obvious, are those whom we have already identified as those who have offended us or sinned against us. Here we find the traditional act of forgiveness that we have come to expect. Keep in mind, however, that this act itself can be difficult, especially when the sin committed against us seems great in the eyes of the world. The greater the perceived level of the sin committed, the more difficult it may be for us to forgive. How could it be that God sees all sin equally, yet we clearly attribute degrees of evil to various types of sin and feel fully justified in doing so? The answer lies in the difference between sin itself and the moral outrage at the consequences of that sin. To God, all sin is equal, because there is only one sin—disobedience. To man, sin carries degrees of severity because the moral consequences of one particular act of disobedience can be more significant than those of another. In order for us to truly forgive as the Lord's Prayer describes, we must learn to forgive in the same way that our Father does and not evaluate the level of moral outrage that was created in order to determine whether or not we will release that forgiveness.

Keep in mind that there are many scriptures that indicate we should forgive those who sin against us, but one in particular is worth examining here. Luke 17:3 indicates that if our brother sins and he repents, then we should forgive him. This passage, when taken out of context and alone, has been used by many to justify the position that there is no obligation to forgive unless the person who sinned chooses repentance. It is worth noting that there is at least some question as to whether or not verse 3 should include the words "against you," and in fact, some translations such as the English Standard Version do not include these words. In that context, our release of forgiveness for sin generally committed requires repentance, but (as indicated in Luke 17:4, where there is no dispute about the inclusion of the words "against you") when the sin is against us personally, no such prerequisite appears to exist.

The second group identified in scripture as needing our forgiveness are those whom we have something against. This does not necessarily mean that these individuals have actually wronged us or sinned against us, but rather that we are offended with them. This group of people is identified when Mark writes his gospel:

> *And whenever you stand praying, forgive, if you have anything against anyone, so that your Father also who is in heaven may forgive you your trespasses.*
>
> Mark 11:25 ESV

The underlying Greek used in this passage actually suggests that we should not only forgive those whom we are offended by, even if they have done us no actual wrong, but that we should also forgive those whom we, for some reason, look down upon.

The third group of people that Scripture indicates is in need of our forgiveness are ourselves. This may be difficult for some to comprehend, but we often hold more offense against ourselves than we do anyone else. It is actually quite easy to see ourselves as having sinned against ourselves and to hold that grudge against our own nature until it destroys us. The scriptural basis for this category of forgiveness is less clear than the others; however, it is quite sufficient to support this understanding.

> *And one of the scribes came up and heard them disputing with one another, and seeing that he answered them well, asked him, "Which commandment is the most important of all?" Jesus answered, "The most important is, 'Hear, O Israel: The Lord our God, the Lord is one. And you shall love the Lord your God with all your heart and with all your soul and with all your mind and with all your strength.' The second is this: 'You shall love your neighbor as yourself.' There is no other commandment greater than these."*
>
> Mark 12:28–31 ESV

Because we most frequently read this passage in the context of considering the two great commandments themselves, we sometimes fail to consider the implications of living the commandments out. This passage identifies three recipients of love: God (v.30), others (neighbor, v. 31), and ourselves (v. 31). If, as it seems to be, it is reasonable to conclude that we cannot love our brother without forgiving him, then we cannot love ourselves without forgiving ourselves. Verse 31 could be paraphrased to read: "You must forgive yourself, just as you must forgive others."

Knowing whom to forgive allows us to make a more complete examination of our hearts to determine whether we have met the standard presented by this prayer's instruction, but we will almost certainly find there are times when we reach a point of believing that we just can't keep giving forgiveness. The repetitive actions of others that wound us, whether it is the same act repeated over and over or a series of different offenses caused over time, can be as significant as the perceived degree of the sin committed. The same scripture that requires forgiveness for those who sin against us also provides insight into whether or not we ever reach a point when we no longer have to extend that forgiveness.

> *Then Peter came up and said to him, "Lord, how often will my brother sin against me, and I forgive him? As many as seven times?" Jesus said to him, "I do not say to you seven times, but seventy times seven."*
> Matthew 18:21–22 ESV

This passage places tremendous expectations upon our ability to forgive. While it is doubtful that many would assume Jesus meant that we only have to forgive our brother 490 times, it is important to understand why Jesus was saying that there should be no end to our forgiveness. In scripture, when the number seven is used, it is often a metaphor for the idea of completion, and when the number seventy is used, it often represents fulfillment. Thus, when asked how often we must forgive, Jesus responded that we must forgive until our forgiveness is utterly and completely fulfilled.

Finally, it is important to remember that forgiving and forgetting are two completely different things. Forgiveness is a choice. However, we cannot simply choose to forget. We were created to be creatures of forgiveness, but not created to be creatures of forgetfulness. The fact that our memories will only fade over time can be a significant hindrance to forgiveness. Our adversary will often harass us with the idea that we have not forgiven because we have not forgotten. Think of forgiveness in this way. We can pick up a bell and begin to ring it. Once the bell has been rung, it cannot be un-rung and the memory of its sound is ingrained upon our mind. However, it is possible to put the bell down and not continue to ring it. When someone has offended us, the offense in us is like picking up a bell and ringing it. We may not be able to forget the pain of the offense or the sound of the bell, but we can choose not to walk in it, to put the bell down and stop ringing it.

Fresh Bread by Michael B. French

While the previous portion of the Lord's Prayer—give us this day our daily bread—may be one of the most difficult to understand, this portion—forgive us our debts, as we forgive our debtors—may be one of the most difficult to walk out. It is important for us to recognize that the life of a believer in Christ was never suggested nor intended to be easy, but instead it was designed to be transformational.

"Forgive us our debts, as we forgive our debtors." We choose to let go of every offense that we have held against those around us. Father, as we forgive, extend Your forgiveness to us. Teach us to completely and utterly release those who have offended us from the liability to which we have held them. We choose to release not only those who have hurt and offended us, and those whom we have held anything against, but also ourselves.

Breaking Bread

Forgive Us Our Debts, As We Forgive Our Debtors
(Matthew 6:12)

EXAMINE

What is a simile or a direct comparison, and why is it important to understand this literary device in order to recognize what Jesus was teaching in this portion of the Lord's Prayer?

_____

_____

_____

_____

Have you ever had difficulty forgiving someone? What, if any, impact has that difficulty had on your life?

_____

_____

_____

How does forgiveness or the lack thereof affect your relationships with others? How does it affect your relationship with God?

_____

_____

_____

_____

Is it possible to maintain an attitude of forgiveness without being able to totally forget the offense? If so, what practical steps can be taken to accomplish this?

_____

_____

_____

_____

REFLECT

Take some time this week to reflect on the phrase "forgive us our debts, as we forgive our debtors" from Matthew 6:12. Reflect on how God has demonstrated His willingness to forgive you—both globally through the sending of His Son, and specifically as applied to your individual life. Set aside at least fifteen minutes to spend just being quiet and listening.

ACT

Take some time this week to actively examine your heart and honestly evaluate whether or not there is anyone against whom you still hold an offense. Identify the offense and take calculated, deliberate steps to let go of it. Make a choice this week to forgive, not as an emotional response toward the individual, but as a decision that honors God, our Father. If needed, discuss your situation with a mature believer who will not enter into offense with you, but help you to overcome your offense.

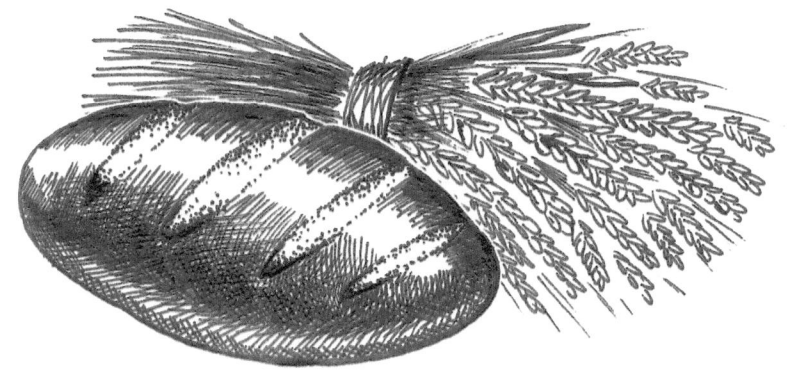

Chapter 9
Lead Us Not into Temptation

At first glance, the phrase "lead us not into temptation" seems straightforward and simple. Certainly the God who created us and loved us enough to send His only Son to die in order that our relationship with Him might be restored would never lead us into a place of temptation. The ideas associated with this phrase seem much more related to a request that God not tempt us to act in a sinful or evil way. Does the inclusion of this portion of the prayer imply that God does at times lead us into temptation? Does this make God a tempter? The real question that must be asked, in order to begin the process of understanding this element of the Lord's Prayer is, what is temptation?

The Greek word translated "temptation" in this passage is *peirasmos* (pi-ras-mos'), which means putting to proof or an experiment, attempt, trial, or proving.[74] The word used in this verse is derived from, but slightly different than, another Greek word, *peirazo* (pi-rad'-zo), which is also translated as temptation in various other passages of the New Testament. This second Greek word means "to test" or "to try or test one's faith, virtue or character, by enticement to sin."[75] The key definitional phrases that distinguishes these two Greek words are the terms *prove* and *entice*.

Who Is the Tempter?

The distinction between *prove* and *entice* is of the utmost importance in determining who plays the role of tempter in our lives. When we understand the distinction, then we understand that God is not the tempter, but rather that role is filled by Satan. When *peirasmos* is used (as it is in the Lord's Prayer), the idea conveyed is much more like taking a test that proves we have an understanding of the subject matter. On the other hand, *peirazo* suggests that a person is being enticed to sin and their faith is being tested in order to find its breaking point. While our Father will certainly engage in *peirasmos* to test us, He is never the originator of *peirazo*. This can be quite confusing when we read the New Testament in virtually any of our English language translations. Consider this description of temptation as written by James:

> *Let no one say when he is tempted, "I am being tempted by God," for God cannot be tempted with evil, and he himself tempts no one. But each person is tempted when he is lured and enticed by his own desire. Then desire when it has conceived gives birth to sin, and sin when it is fully grown brings forth death.*
>
> James 1:13–15 ESV

Our adversary, the devil, is hard at work attempting to bring about the destruction of our faith and the eradication of our relationship with our Father. According to James, the process that he uses is to tempt mankind in an effort to lure us away, entice us by our own soulish desires, and bring forth sin as a fruit of that union. The end result, as indicated both in this passage from James and by Paul in Romans 6:23, is death.

There can be no doubt that this is not something God undertakes in our lives. Jesus made this distinction abundantly clear when He declared, "The thief comes only to steal and kill and destroy. I came that they may have life and have it abundantly."[76] Jesus gives life; the enemy takes life. Jesus builds up; the enemy tears down. Jesus gives; the enemy takes. Satan is the tempter, and this provides what seems to be a simple, surface-level explanation for why Jesus included the phrase, "Lead us not into temptation," in the Lord's Prayer. Yet, with just a little thought, this surface explanation begins to fall apart.

If God is not a tempter and He tempts no one, then it is difficult to believe that He would ever stoop to semantics and instead of actually tempting us Himself, lead us into a place where we will be tempted by our adversary. To lead us to a place of temptation offers very little distinction from God tempting us Himself. Embracing the surface understanding of this phrase would seem to lend itself more to an instructional prayer that asks God to keep us from temptation, rather than to lead us not into temptation. Since asking God not to lead us into temptation (testing that proves our understanding) suggests that there may be times when He does, it is imperative that we look deeper to find the meaning behind these words of Jesus.

Who Is the Tester?

While our adversary may be the tempter, it is our Father God who is the tester. We already know, from the examination of the phrase "give us this day, our daily bread," that God is not opposed to testing us to see whether we will obey the instructions that He gives to us.[77] Just as with the New Testament word translated as "temptation" in the Lord's Prayer, the psalmist makes clear, by actually asking for his heart and mind to be tested, that the purpose of God's testing in the Old Testament was to prove us.[78]

Deuteronomy 8:2 indicates that the entire forty-year period in the wilderness was a time for God to test the children of Israel that He might know what was in their hearts. In Jeremiah 17:10, we find the Lord searching the heart and testing the mind of man to give every man according to his ways or, as the Living Bible puts it, "so he can give to each person his right reward."

Since the Lord already knows the secrets of our hearts,[79] He doesn't need to search it or test us to find out what is going on. Instead, it seems that God searches and tests so that we can come to know what is in our own hearts and minds and be transformed as they are renewed.

> *Do not be conformed to this world, but be transformed by the renewal of your mind, that by testing you may discern what is the will of God, what is good and acceptable and perfect.*
>
> Romans 12:2 ESV

While the Greek word translated as "testing" here is not the same as that translated as "temptation" in the Lord's Prayer, it is a word that also means "to test or prove."[80] In other words, the Lord will test us, so that we can learn who we are and compare that to the will of God for us, thus being transformed more into His image.

This is far different from the tempting or testing that our adversary thrusts upon us. In fact, this type of testing is explained by James as being so profitable to us that it should be welcomed in our lives.

> *Count it all joy, my brothers, when you meet trials of various kinds, for you know that the testing of your faith produces steadfastness. And let steadfastness have its full effect, that you may be perfect and complete, lacking in nothing.*
>
> James 1:2–4 ESV

The word translated as "testing" here is the same one used in Romans that means "to put to proof," just like *peirasmos* from the Lord's Prayer. James is telling us that we should be joyful when we fall into temptation or testing because it is going to be an experiment that proves our faith and brings forth maturity. While this may affirm that the kind of testing that Jesus and James spoke of is far different from that which our adversary engages in, it does raise a new question: Why does James tell us to welcome it and Jesus teach us to pray that we might not be led into it?

Reconciling the teaching of Jesus in Matthew 6:13 with James 1:2–4 is simply a matter of understanding whether we are being led into the temptation by God or whether it is overtaking us along our journey. Paul gives his explanation of such *peirasmos* temptation when he writes his first letter to the Corinthians.

> *No temptation has overtaken you that is not common to man. God is faithful, and he will*

> *not let you be tempted beyond your ability, but with the temptation he will also provide the way of escape, that you may be able to endure it.*
>
> 1 Corinthians 10:13 ESV

Jesus teaches that we should pray not to be led into temptation, while Paul describes temptation as overtaking us. Paul goes on to explain that no temptation that overtakes us will be beyond our ability to handle or without a way to escape. Together, Jesus, Paul, and James help us understand what Jesus was teaching in the Lord's Prayer.

Jesus' language, "lead us not into temptation," presumes that all the previous lines of His prayer have been prayed and understood. By the time we reach this phrase, we have already prayed:

- *That God's name be sanctified in us*
- *That the Kingdom be revealed through us*
- *That the will of God be manifest in us*
- *That we are provided with what we need each day to fulfill these tasks, and*
- *That we walk as forgivers who are partakers of forgiveness.*

If these characteristics are taking root in our lives, then God need not lead us into temptation, because each day will provide enough to overtake us that we can take joy in overcoming and being transformed more fully into the image of Christ.

Perhaps we could understand this element of the Lord's Prayer more clearly to be: *Lord, let every temptation that overtakes us prove that Your perfect will is still being worked in us and that we are growing more perfect through every test that we pass. Keep us in a place where we don't have to have You lead us into them, but where we gain what we need from each one we encounter.*

Jesus was teaching us to pray that we would have a sufficient relationship with the Father that the testing of our faith was no longer something He must position us to walk into. He would later teach His disciples to "watch and pray that you may not enter into temptation. The spirit indeed is willing, but the flesh is weak."[81] This goal should be ever-present in our minds and sought by our spirits, but it is important to note that our flesh is weak and temptation will continue to pursue us. With each test we successfully pass, we are strengthened and the willingness of our soul to submit in obedience to our spirit is increased. It is for this reason that overcoming temptation requires us to watch and pray. Recognizing that the disciples were asleep when Jesus confronted them in Matthew 26, we can also then understand the Lord's Prayer as teaching us to ask God to *wake us up!*

"Lead us not into temptation." O God, wake us up! Train us and teach us, so that we would quickly pass the tests You set before us and grow into the maturity displayed by living up to the full measure of Your stature. Prepare us that we would quickly identify the temptations of the enemy and turn away because we have already learned from Your testing how to avoid such schemes.

Breaking Bread

Lead Us Not into Temptation
(Matthew 6:13)

EXAMINE

What is the difference between temptation and testing, and what is the purpose of each in your life as a Christian?

_____

_____

_____

_____

Have you ever walked through a time when you felt like God was testing you? What, if anything, did you learn from that season?

_____

_____

_____

_____

Is it really possible to maintain joy during a time of testing? Is there a difference between joy and happiness, and if so, does such a distinction help you during a period of testing?

___

___

___

___

What is the role of prayer in helping us to overcome testing/temptation? How has your personal prayer life helped you in this area?

___

___

___

___

REFLECT

Take some time this week to reflect on the phrase "lead us not into temptation" from Matthew 6:13. Reflect on how God has used seasons of testing in your life to strengthen you. Consider both the times when these experiences have succeeded and the times when they have failed to initiate spiritual growth. What made the experiences different? Set aside at least fifteen minutes to spend just being quiet and listening.

ACT

Take some time this week to determine the season of life that you are in (i.e., a season of testing, temptation, or stability). Once you have identified the season, take time to consider how you can respond to what God is doing at this moment in your life. Write down five ways you can respond in cooperation with what God is currently doing in you. Chose one of these responses to focus on each day this week and take deliberate action in cooperation with what God is doing. If necessary, discuss your situation with a more mature believer to help identify both the season you are in and the ways you can respond.

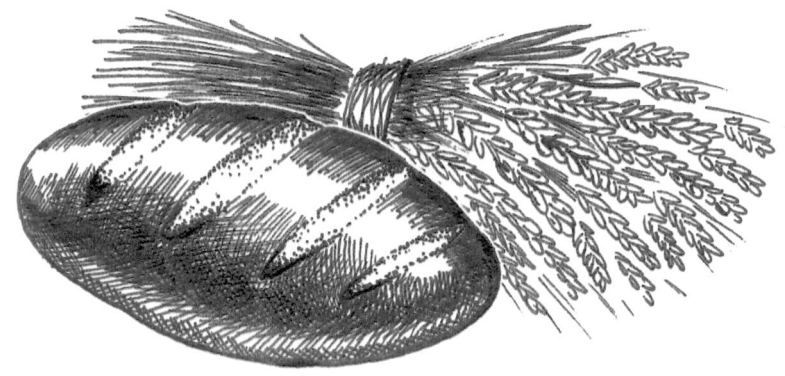

Chapter 10
But Deliver Us from Evil

As we examined the instruction to pray that God would not lead us into temptation, that examination brought us to the understanding that there are two different types of temptation. The first is brought about by God to prove us, and the second is thrust upon us by the enemy to destroy us. While the words "lead us not into temptation" dealt with the proof that God desires to extract from our lives, the phrase "deliver us from evil" deals with the destruction that our adversary wishes to rain down upon us. The conjunction "but" stands between these two phrases, used to introduce something that contrasts with that which has already been mentioned. While we want God to help us wake up and reach a level of maturity where His character is constantly displayed in our lives, we also need Him to keep us safe from the traps and snares of the enemy, who is out to keep us from that destiny.

The Greek word *rhuomai* (hroo'-om-ahee), which is translated as "deliver," literally means "to rescue from or to preserve from."[82] This word is for the most part synonymous with the Greek term *sozo* (sode'-zo), which means to save. The primary difference is that *rhuomai*, as used in the Lord's Prayer, emphasizes rescue, while *sozo* emphasizes preservation.[83] The choice of words that Jesus made was not by accident. Since we were all born into sin, then we, by our sin nature, have a tendency to be ensnared by the enemy's traps. Jesus recognized that it would not be unusual, nor even uncommon, to find ourselves caught in those snares; thus He taught us to pray that we might be rescued from them.

Luke records the prophecy of Zechariah at the birth of his son, John the Baptist, as declaring that Jesus would deliver us from the hand of our enemies, so that we could serve God without fear.[84] Paul explains that when we become followers of Jesus, God delivers us from the power of darkness and places us into the Kingdom of His Son.[85] Certainly these passages make clear that when we are born again, we are delivered from the hand of the enemy. If this is true, then why would Jesus teach His disciples, those who believed in Him, to continue praying for such deliverance?

Paul wrote to Timothy that he had been rescued or delivered from the lion's mouth (though perhaps a literal event, this is also a metaphor for being set free from Satan and brought into the Kingdom of God). He went on to then declare that because of that experience, he was confident that the Lord would rescue or deliver him from every evil deed, thus preserving him until He came safely into His heavenly Kingdom.[86] Paul's letter suggests that although we have been delivered from the enemy's kingdom generally, we continue to need rescue from his ongoing traps. So just what are these evil deeds that we need to be delivered from?

The word Jesus chose to describe evil suggests that it is a series of things full of labors, annoyances, and hardships, or a bad nature or condition.[87] The enemy is crafty and there are many ways he seeks to entrap us. Jesus wanted us to be free from all of them. While this prayer could certainly be recognized as an affirmation of the ministry of deliverance, which is being rescued from demonic influence and control, overcoming the traps of these evil spirits[88] is by no means the only place from which we are taught to seek rescue.[89] Other passages suggest several other annoyances or conditions from which we should seek God's assistance for our rescue.

Our Nature

There is an ongoing battle between our soul and our spirit, even after we have been born again. Our soul, consisting of our mind, will, and emotions, does not desire to give up the control that it exercised prior to salvation. The old man, or old nature, is considered evil in scripture, and we should seek God's help to be free from its influence.

> *For no good tree bears bad fruit, nor again does a bad tree bear good fruit, for each tree is known by its own fruit. For figs are not gathered from thornbushes, nor are grapes picked from a bramble bush. The good person out of the good treasure of his heart produces good, and the evil person out of his evil treasure produces evil, for out of the abundance of the heart his mouth speaks.*
>
> Luke 6:43–45 ESV

Our nature is known by the fruit our lives produce. While each of us who are in Christ is a new creation, with old things having passed away,[90] the battle for the control of our nature continues to rage. Bob Jones, a dear prophetic friend, was known to explain it this way: "The old man may be dead, but every now and then he tries to climb up out of that grave. When that happens, you just need to get a shovel and beat him back down." When we pray "deliver us from evil," we are asking God to show us where the shovel is and rescue us from the attempts of our old nature to regain control of our lives.

Our Reputation

Generally speaking, our reputation is reflected in the beliefs or opinions that others hold about us. In other words, it is the appearance we present to those around us. A very familiar passage from 1 Thessalonians 5:22 instructs us to "abstain from all appearance of evil." As believers, it is important that we guard our reputations and preserve them from the evil influences of the enemy. Other translations say we should abstain from every form of evil. When people look at our lives, they are not drawn into a renewed relationship with our Father by seeing either a good or an evil personal reputation; instead, they are drawn nearer to Him by seeing Jesus reflected in us. However, in order for Jesus to be seen in us, a godly reputation is desirable.

Paul suggested a manner of cultivating a godly reputation when he wrote to the Philippians:

> *Finally, brothers, whatever is true, whatever is honorable, whatever is just, whatever is pure, whatever is lovely, whatever is commendable, if there is any excellence, if there is anything worthy of praise, think about these things. What you have learned and received and heard and seen in me— practice these things, and the God of peace will be with you.*
>
> Philippians 4:8–9 ESV

Some may ask how this scripture relates to our reputation. This is a principle of meditation that allows us to know and experience the peace of God. While that is true, verse 5 of this same chapter begins with the words, "Let all men know and perceive and recognize..."[91] This is one of those places where the words that follow vary widely from translation to translation.

"Let all men know and perceive and recognize..."

KJV	"...your moderation..."
NKJV/NIV	"...your gentleness..."
ESV	"...your reasonableness..."
ASV/RSV	"...your forbearance..."
AMP	"...your unselfishness, considerateness, forbearing..."

Regardless of the translation, this passage is declaring that we should guard what people see in our lives. The word that gives such a wide range of translations is *epieikes* (ep-ee-i-kace'), which basically means seemly or suitable.[92] We are to let all men see that we are suitable for the Kingdom lifestyle, that our reputation points to Jesus and not to ourselves. One of the ways we guard that reputation is to meditate on those things that are true, honorable, just, pure, lovely, commendable, excellent, and worthy of praise.

When we are praying as instructed in the Lord's Prayer, we are asking God to set us free from our own reputation, so that His light and His love might be seen in us. To pray this prayer as it was intended, we are actually asking God to refocus our attention so that those principles of Philippians 4:8–9 are not only things that we meditate on, but things that we begin to display for others to see and be drawn to Jesus.

Our Character

Our character is slightly different from our reputation. Reputation is based upon the belief or opinion of others about us. Character reflects the moral qualities distinctly applicable to us, regardless of any other person's opinions. The quality of having strong moral principles or of walking uprightly is known as *integrity*. God has called us to be a people of the highest character who walk in great integrity. However, the world—at the direction of our enemy—seeks to corrupt that character and destroy our integrity. This tendency toward evil defiles us and suggests yet another area where we need to be rescued by our Father in order to fulfill our destiny. In the Gospel of Mark, Jesus describes this natural state of man that must be overcome:

> *For from within, out of the heart of man, come evil thoughts, sexual immorality, theft, murder, adultery, coveting, wickedness, deceit, sensuality, envy, slander, pride, foolishness. All these evil things come from within, and they defile a person.*
>
> Mark 7:21–23 ESV

Our nature prior to our salvation tends to promote exactly these things and inhibit the growth of true character. Salvation affords us the opportunity to overcome our old nature, but we must also take that opportunity to build up the character and integrity that will sustain us on our Kingdom journey. To this end we need deliverance from the evil that corrupts our character. Paul wrote to the Ephesians and advised them that they must be careful in how they walk, that they must guard their journey with wisdom because the days are evil.[93]

Our character is like light that comes from deep within us, revealing who we truly are. If that light is dim or even dark, we can attempt to bolster it by drawing on our reputation; however, our core nature will ultimately be the deciding factor in what others discern about us. We must let the light or character of God (for He is light, according to 1 John 1:5) shine forth and be set free from any evil that darkens it or hides it from others:

> *No one after lighting a lamp puts it in a cellar or under a basket, but on a stand, so that those who enter may see the light. Your eye is the lamp of your body. When your eye is healthy, your whole body is full of light, but when it is bad, your body is full of darkness. Therefore be careful lest the light in you be darkness. If then your whole body is full of light, having no part dark, it will be wholly bright, as when a lamp with its rays gives you light.*
>
> Luke 11:33–36 ESV

When we pray this portion of the Lord's Prayer, we are asking to be free from the cellar—for God to take the basket off—so that we can display the very heart of who we are rather than being dependent upon our reputation to suggest who we might be.

"Deliver us from evil." Set us free from the lingering effects of our previous sin nature. Rescue us from the reputations that we have built for ourselves, so that nothing stands between the light of God within us and the world around us. Make us a people of character and integrity, so that we can be used by You.

Breaking Bread

Deliver Us from Evil
(Matthew 6:13)

EXAMINE

Is there some area in your life where you currently need God to rescue you? Consider the difference between "rescue" and "preservation" as you answer.

_____

_____

_____

_____

What role does fear play in overcoming your old man? Is there any area in your life where fear has hindered you from becoming the person God created you to be?

_____

_____

_____

_____

What type of reputation do you have? Whether it is good or bad, does it dictate any of your choices in life as you attempt to maintain it or overcome it? If so, how?

_____

_____

_____

_____

How does the Lord Jesus see you? Describe yourself using only language that reflects how God views you and the destiny for which He has created you.

_____

_____

_____

_____

REFLECT

Take some time this week to reflect on the phrase "deliver us from evil" from Matthew 6:13. Reflect on how God has transformed your life since you accepted Christ as your personal Savior. Set aside at least fifteen minutes to spend just being quiet and listening.

ACT

Take some time this week to actively examine your life and consider what aspects of your old (pre-Christian) nature are still being displayed. Identify a single area where your old nature continues to rule you. Seek God this week and petition heaven to deliver you from that aspect of your character. Identify and write down five action points that the Lord reveals to you that will help you to overcome that aspect of your identity. Seek ways to implement one action point each day this week.

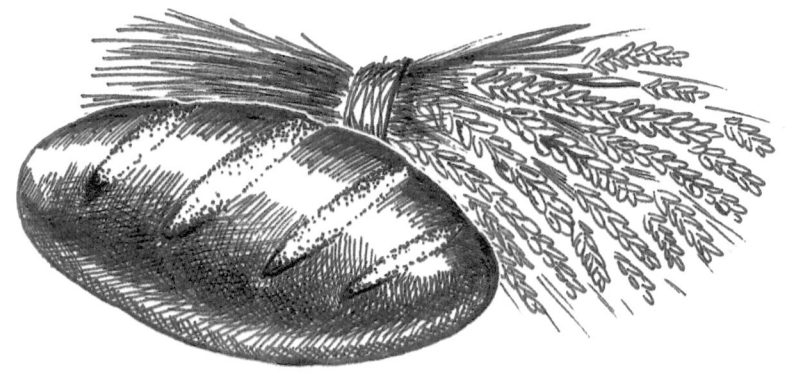

Chapter 11
Kingdom, Power, and Glory

Augustine was perhaps the first to suggest that the Lord's Prayer consists of seven petitions. The first three of these petitions relate to eternity, while the last four concern the temporal. Recognizing that eternity has already begun and that we should be living a Kingdom life in the here and now, it might be more appropriate to consider the first three petitions as concerning our spiritual responsibilities, while the latter four concern the issues that need to be addressed in order to fulfill them. By this view, the first words, "our Father in heaven," establish an introduction that helps us know whom we are praying to and where He can be found. The final phrase, "for Yours is the kingdom and the power and the glory forever," is omitted from Augustine's evaluation, just as it is omitted from many translations of God's Word. It would be helpful to summarize these seven petitions, prior to examining where the final phrase originates and why it is included when we pray the Lord's Prayer.

The Three Spiritual Responsibilities
The first two verses in the Lord's Prayer outline our spiritual responsibilities: 1) to make God's name holy, 2) to express the fullness of His Kingdom for the earth to see, and 3) to reveal His will in a manner the earth can recognize.

While these are spiritual responsibilities that relate to eternity, they are necessary in this present age to bring heaven into the earth. They are not expressions for the distant future, but responsibilities we have a part in fulfilling in the here and now. As we have learned, it is impossible for us to fulfill any one of these responsibilities in our own strength, and by necessity we must petition our Father to fulfill them in us and through us. In these three areas, we ask our Father to reveal Himself to the earth by using us, the body of Christ, as His instruments.

We are both individual members whom God uses to reveal Himself and, collectively, one body who has partaken of fresh bread together.[94] Having done so, we are becoming a unified picture of our Father, whose name we bear. Keep in mind as we seek to bear these spiritual responsibilities that while we are one body, each of us has different gifts, different callings, and different ways in which we fulfill them.[95] The Lord's Prayer is not only a prayer that we can memorize and pray together in unison as one body, it is also a prayer filled with individual petitions for God to reveal Himself in each of us individually.

The Four Issues to Be Addressed
Matthew 6:11-13 outlines the four areas that we petition for God to address in our lives so that we may meet the responsibilities outlined by the first two verses. These areas of need include: 1) provide what we need to fulfill our destiny, 2) teach us to forgive so that we can walk in forgiveness, 3) help us mature so that You don't have to continue testing us, and 4) rescue us from our old nature, our present reputation, and our poor character so that we can be free from all of the enemy's influence in our lives.

These final four petitions are cries for God to bring about transformation in our lives so that we can truly become who we were created to be. Do we expect to be able to truly make His name known in the earth and to show forth His holiness through our lives? Do we, as His sons, actually expect to carry His name? Do we expect to make His Kingdom visible through what we say and do? Do we expect not only to see His will done in a sovereign way that acknowledges His control over all things, but specifically in and through our lives and in those specific places our feet touch?

If we truly expect these things, then we must seek out the fresh bread for each day and hear His voice for our immediate circumstances so that He becomes our very present help in trouble[96] and our Provider of grace in time of need.[97] We must learn to walk in forgiveness—both given and received—so that we might live an overcomer's life appropriating the victory we have already attained through Christ's triumph over the works of darkness.[98] We must learn to live our lives in such a way that our faith is real and put to use each day, not requiring that God test us in order for it to be strengthened, but exercised regularly (like the very muscles of our body) as we live this life.[99] We must have our very nature changed, so that we are no longer subject to the devil, but walk in the character and integrity associated with God our Father.[100]

Kingdom, Power, and Glory

With these things in mind, we can consider the final words of the Lord's Prayer. Perhaps you have wondered why these words are so common when we recite the prayer, yet frequently absent when we read it in a context outside of the King James Version of the Bible. The reason is because the words, "for Yours is the kingdom and the power and the glory forever," while found in most Greek manuscripts, were not contained in the main body of the *Critical Text* from which most translations are taken. The King James Version and the New King James Version, which include these words, were based upon the *Textus Receptus*.

These words have become known as the doxology (prayer of praise) and were contained in and possibly introduced by the *Diadache* ("teaching," one of the earliest Christian documents probably compiled before the end of the first century) written between 70 AD and 140 AD (minus "the kingdom," which was added around 250 to 380 AD). The words were added by believers in the early Church as a closing phrase for the prayer. If added, they almost certainly were not intended as an addition to the prayer, but rather as an acknowledgment that none of the things prayed can be done by us alone—that it is only through God, whose Kingdom it is, whose power it is, and who deserves all of the glory that this prayer might be fulfilled.

Regardless of whether this phrase is found in the original prayer or was added by early Christians, its value is without dispute and is certainly consistent with established scripture in 1 Chronicles 29:10–13.

It is essential that we remember, as we delve into tasting to see that the Lord is good[101] by partaking of this fresh bread, that none of it is possible without Him. He is our Creator, Provider, Healer, and Strength. In any petition that we lift before our Father, whether it be the exact words of the Lord's Prayer or petitions prayed in recognition of the lessons learned from it, we must give honor where honor is due.

Fresh Bread by Michael B. French

"Yours is the kingdom and the power and the glory forever." Father, we acknowledge You and all that You have done for us. We recognize that we have eternal spiritual responsibilities that require our lives to be transformed in order for us to fulfill them. It is only in You that we have hope to fulfill this purpose. It is Your Kingdom that sets the stage for our response, Your power that enables our response, and Your glory that our response reveals.

Breaking Bread

Kingdom, Power, and Glory
(Matthew 6:13)

EXAMINE

How has recognizing the spiritual responsibilities that God has given you affected your daily walk with God?

_____

_____

_____

_____

Have you noticed any transformation in your life as you have examined and prayed the Lord's Prayer with deeper understanding? If so, describe your experience.

_____

_____

_____

_____

In what ways can your life present a clearer picture of God's Kingdom? Display His power? Bring Him more glory?

_____

_____

_____

_____

Does the fact that the phrase "yours is the kingdom and the power and the glory forever" may have been added later to the original text have any effect—positive or negative—upon your view of its significance?

_____

_____

_____

_____

REFLECT

Take some time this week to reflect on the phrase "yours is the kingdom and the power and the glory forever." Reflect on what these words mean and what they say about the One to whom you are praying. Set aside at least fifteen minutes to spend just being quiet and listening.

ACT

Consider how you can be a part of establishing God's Kingdom, displaying His power, and/or bringing Him glory this week. Write down five practical ways that you can accomplish one of these tasks. Choose one way that you identified and focus your attention this week upon living it out. Share the testimony of any success you have with a friend and encourage them so that they, too, can reflect God's Kingdom, power, and glory on the earth.

Fresh Bread by Michael B. French

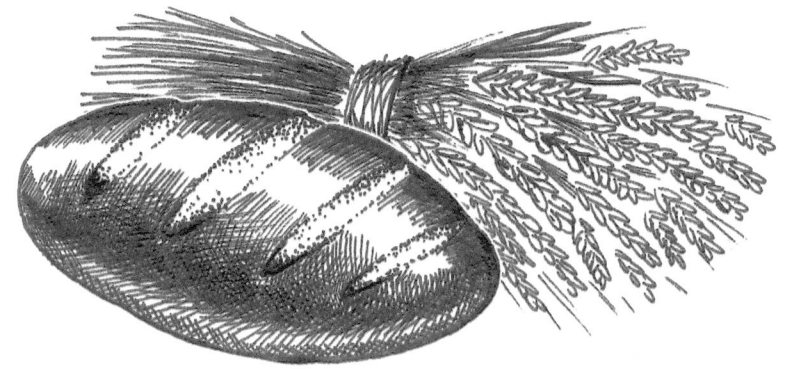

Chapter 12
Amen

Let us not forsake the final word of the Lord's Prayer, "Amen." This is the word that closes not only the Lord's Prayer, but most of our prayers, and yet we rarely consider it at all. What is the implication of closing our prayers with the term "amen"? Does it mean anything at all, or is it simply a way of saying that the prayer is finished? Working on the premise that not a single word included in scripture is without significance, there must be some reason that it would be included here in even a few of the English translations of this passage.

While we may think little about it, most of us will recognize that to say "amen" is to say "so be it," but it also means "may it be fulfilled."[102] To close our prayer in this fashion indicates that we are agreeing with God that what we have asked will be accomplished. According to Matthew 18:19, if any two of us agree on earth about anything, then our Father in heaven will do it. While Jesus left the earth to ascend to heaven, He did not leave us without a representative present on the earth. In fact, in John 14:15–17, Jesus specifically promised that another Helper—the Holy Spirit—would be with us forever. By teaching us how to pray through the Lord's Prayer, Jesus was instructing us in how to ask God rightly so that we could have what we ask for (see James 4:2–3). When we ask rightly (asking for the very things God Himself puts in our hearts) and we ask in agreement (when asking rightly we are at minimum in agreement with the Holy Spirit), then we should expect to receive.

Finally, it important for us to understand how amazing God is, not only in teaching us through the Lord's Prayer, but also in understanding the implications of how we would choose to use it. As we have seen, God never intended that this prayer become a ritualistic, repetitive prayer that would simply be recited for generations without understanding. Or did He? What appears to be a paradox to man is often just a part of God's plan that rises to a level beyond our current understanding. In fact, it seems that God had great purpose in allowing the Lord's Prayer to be memorized and prayed repetitively. Since the time that Jesus taught it, countless millions have prayed this prayer without fail over centuries of time. The atmosphere, both spiritual and natural, has been flooded with these petitions, and while man may not have always understood what he was praying, he has indeed prayed in accordance with the will of God and asked for exactly what Jesus instructed us to do. According to 1 John 5:14–15, if we ask anything according to His will, He hears us and if we know He hears us, then we also know that we are going to receive what we have asked for. While we may have asked with the wrong motives at times (James 4:3), the repetitive nature of how we have used this prayer has never allowed it to waver from the instructions that Jesus gave.

Consider then, that for over 2,000 years, believers have prayed this prayer in agreement and according to the will of God. God has heard it and is still hearing it, and there is little doubt that in these last days He is answering it. He is preparing a people to reveal His holiness, carry His name, fulfill His will, and demonstrate His Kingdom on the earth. He is teaching His children to see the world through His own eyes, allowing forgiveness to reign in our midst; to trust Him for enough of His light to fulfill our destiny each day; and to guard our steps in such a way that we walk free from the traps and snares of the enemy and mature into the sons of God we were created to be. Generations have prayed for us, even as we pray for the next generation, and it is time for the fruit of those prayers to be brought forth.

Breaking Bread

Amen
(Matthew 6:13)

EXAMINE

What does it mean to "come into agreement" with God? Is it really possible to agree in prayer with the Holy Spirit? If so, how?

_____

_____

_____

_____

Are ritual/memorized prayers positive or negative? Does the Lord's Prayer have any impact when it is prayed simply as repetitious words?

_____

_____

_____

_____

How can your motives affect your ability to come into agreement with God when you pray?

What impact, if any, does knowing that God wants to put His desires within you, for you to pray back to Him and in agreement with Him, have on your prayer life?

REFLECT

Take some time this week to reflect on the word "amen." Consider your prayer life and whether it is personal or impersonal in its nature. Set aside at least fifteen minutes to spend just being quiet and listening.

ACT

Practice making your prayers more personal this week. Write down five ways that you can interact with heaven as you pray, avoiding clichés, habitual responses, and repetitive phrases. Focus each day this week on praying in agreement with God and overcoming the temptation to pray in any manner that has become habitual for you. Write down a one-paragraph summary of how your prayer life was changed by this exercise and share it with those whom you are studying with.

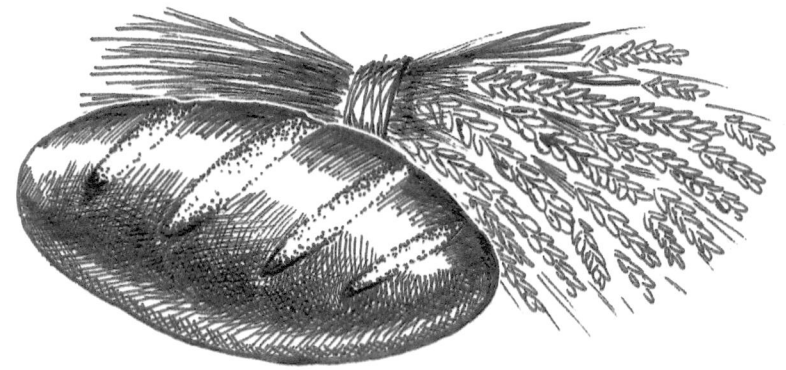

Conclusion

There is a Baker who bakes a special loaf of bread for you each day, and that Baker is *"our Father."* He wants us to know that though He is *"in heaven,"* He is not far from us and that He desires a personal connection with us. He knows exactly the kind of bread we need in order to establish just such a relationship, and the aroma of that bread draws us into the bakery itself. Here the Baker is kneading a part of Himself into every loaf that is baked, and through that bread He shares Himself with us.

By choosing to receive that bread, His very nature is made a part of who we are and we are prepared to *"make His name holy."* When we partake of the bread He has made for us, the nourishment it provides brightens our countenance and others can see *"His Kingdom come."* But He doesn't just hand us the bread and walk away. Instead, He invites us to sit at His table and dine with Him, getting to know Him more as we fellowship. As we listen to Him talk, we grow to know Him more and to more quickly recognize His voice, allowing *"His will to be done"* in us and through us. This great Baker is also a Master Teacher and desires that we would not simply sit back and watch, but that we should touch the dough ourselves and become participants in the baking process, allowing what is accomplished in the bakery to be done *"on earth as it is in heaven."*

What we have seen the Baker do, we also can do. Though we had no money, He has freely chosen to give us His bread to eat, and we can freely choose to give away what we have been given. He has *"forgiven us our debts, as we forgive our debtors."* All this He does with the full knowledge that there will be times when we are tempted to taste of other foods, some of which may even be poison to our lives. He does not *"lead us into temptation,"* but He does provide a continuous supply of His bread to ensure that we know the difference. The Baker offers such fine bread and its taste is so good that we begin to lose all interest in any other foods, and thus He *"delivers us from evil."*

Fresh bread is the best bread! When we are drawn into the presence of the Master Baker by the aroma of freshly baked bread, our appetite is whetted and we become much more aware of those hunger pangs we have been feeling. We can't help but take a bite of what is being offered to us, and when we do, we will never again be satisfied with anything less than fresh, living bread. And when we eat fresh bread long enough, we can't help but build a relationship with the Baker. The Lord's Prayer is not just a prayer—it never has been. It is something more. It is an aroma of bread baking in the ovens of heaven. Jesus spoke these words to whet our appetite and to invite us to become partakers of His glory.[103] We have savored the aroma long enough; now it's time to find your daily portion, take a bite, and see just how good God is!

Fresh Bread by Michael B. French

Review Request

I hope you have gained some insight about the Lord's Prayer and how it can refresh you daily through this book.

Now that you've read *Fresh Bread*, if you enjoyed it, then please let other readers know. Let's share the knowledge and help people to grow and step into the will of the Lord.

About the Author

After practicing law for ten years, Michael received his call into the ministry. Over the past three decades, he has passionately ministered all around the globe. Michael is the founder of Cahaba Equipping Center, a ministry devoted to training and equipping leaders around the world. Michael is also the co-founder and executive director of Patria Ministries, an international association of churches, ministries, and businesses headquartered in Birmingham, Alabama. Michael and his wife, Elisa, live in Leeds, Alabama, with their four sons, Joshua, Caleb, Jacob, and Noah.

Other Books by Michael B. French

Remedy: Freedom Through Deliverance
2014 Readers' Favorite Bronze Award

Deliverance ministry is a touchy subject. Just mention the word *deliverance* and many people conjure up images of *The Exorcist* and other media stereotypes. At a time when the world is confused about deliverance, *Remedy* offers insights on the true authority that Christ intends every believer to walk in. Written by renowned experts Michael and Bill French, this book covers foundational elements and applications of deliverance ministry and includes real-life experiences over their sixty-plus combined years of ministry. The foreword by John Paul Jackson emphasizes the spiritual authority that believers wield in the war raging in people's lives.

Fresh Bread by Michael B. French

The Elisha Way: Preparing for the Double Portion

2013 Readers' Favorite Bronze Award

The generation today has the opportunity to experience the power and presence of God in a way that no other generation before them has. They are an Elisha generation on the brink of taking up their mantle and walking in a double anointing.

Paul wrote the following words to the church in Corinth: "For though you might have ten thousand instructors in Christ, yet you do not have many fathers; for in Christ Jesus I have begotten you through the gospel" (1 Corinthians 4:15 (NKJV).

If we are to once again experience a generational increase in anointing and authority, then it is imperative that we move toward a new form of discipleship—fathering.

Fresh Bread by Michael B. French

About Patria Ministries

www.patriamin.com

Patria is a Greek word used three times in the New Testament (Luke 2:4, Acts 3:25, and Ephesians 3:15), and translated as "linage, kindred, or family." The word itself speaks of paternal descent—that is, it refers to a group of families or a whole race or nation.

> *For this reason I bow my knees to the Father of our Lord Jesus Christ, from whom the whole family in heaven and earth is named.*
> Ephesians 3:14–15 NKJV

Vine's explains this reference in Ephesians as relating to all those who are spiritually related to God the Father and thus being united to one another in "family" fellowship. *Thayer's* indicates that the word is used for a race, tribe, or group of families, all of whom lay claim to a common origin.

Patria Ministries is an association of churches, ministries, and businesses with a common vision. Although each may have its own distinctive purpose (just as each individual member of a family has his or her own distinct identity), we are connected by our common strand of spiritual DNA.

Churches have long been considered families, but when it comes to relationships among churches and ministries (and certainly among churches, ministries, and businesses), governmental and denominational mind-sets have often won the day. It is our desire that Patria Ministries extend the concept of family upward as we relate to one another as a clan or tribe of families striving together to advance the Kingdom of God our Father.

For more information about membership, please see the Patria Ministries website at www.patriamin.com.

Acknowledgments

This book would not have been possible without the help and support of a number of people who knowingly or unknowingly co-labored with me to allow it to come to fruition.

At the forefront of my list would be my amazing wife, who always sees the potential in what I am doing well before I realize it. Without her support and encouragement, I doubt this book would have ever made it off of my journal pages and sermon notes to find its way into your hand.

My four sons, Joshua, Caleb, Jacob, and Noah, have also endured my late-night and early morning meditations and musings when the slightest interruption would sometimes get a slightly harsher response than intended.

I can't forget to thank the people of The Bridge Birmingham, where I was the pastor for seventeen years. They listened, encouraged, and provided me with the responses that enhanced my understanding of what began as a twelve-week sermon series and ended up, more than five years later, as the book you are currently reading. One of those members, Cande Maxie, deserves special attention, as she labored through the reading of the roughest of rough drafts to provide a pre-edited version of this work before it was delivered to my publisher.

And finally, I owe a huge debt of gratitude to Jennifer Minigh, her husband, David, and everyone at ShadeTree Publishing who have believed in me and endured with me to take what I hear in my spirit and transfer it in a readable form to the pages of a book for the third time now.

To all of you, and probably many more whom I have not named, words are not enough to express my gratitude. Please know that you share in any success that may be achieved in advancing the Kingdom of God through the words and teaching contained in this book.

Fresh Bread by Michael B. French

Scriptures and References

[1] Ecclesiastes 1:9 , NKJV
[2] Jeremiah 6:16 , NKJV
[3] 2 Corinthians 5:17
[4] Psalm 34:8 NKJV
[5] NT:3962—*Thayer's Greek Lexicon*, PC Study Bible formatted Electronic Database. Copyright © 2006 by Biblesoft, Inc. All rights reserved.
[6] The ESV footnote to John 3:3 says, "Or from above; the Greek is purposely ambiguous and can mean both again and from above."
[7] 2 Corinthians 5:17
[8] Matthew 5:43–45
[9] Matthew 5:46–48
[10] John 3:16 , ESV
[11] Mark 12:31
[12] 1 John 4:20
[13] Matthew 7:11
[14] Biblesoft's *New Exhaustive Strong's Numbers and Concordance with Expanded Greek-Hebrew Dictionary.* Copyright © 1994, 2003, 2006 Biblesoft, Inc. and International Bible Translators, Inc.
[15] Genesis 3:8
[16] 1 Corinthians 6:19 NKJV
[17] NT:37, "hallow," from *Vine's Expository Dictionary of Biblical Words*, Copyright © 1985, Thomas Nelson Publishers.
[18] T. Herbert Bindley, MA, DD, *St. Cyprian on The Lord's Prayer, An English Translation, with Introduction* (London: Society for Promoting Christian Knowledge, 1914), 38.
[19] Cyril of Alexandria, Commentary on Luke Sermon LXXII *Upon "Hallowed be Your Name"* (1859).
[20] 1 Peter 1:15–16 NKJV; see also Leviticus 19:2
[21] Exodus 3:14 ESV
[22] Galatians 3:26
[23] John 1 and Revelation 19:11–13
[24] John 14:12
[25] Matthew 10:7
[26] Acts 8:12; 19:8

[27] Manlio Simonetti, ed., *Ancient Christian Commentary on Scripture,* vol. New Testament Ia, Matthew 1–13 (Downers Grove, IL: InterVarsity Press, 2001), 131.
[28] Ibid., 131.
[29] 2 Corinthians 4:3–4 ESV
[30] Romans 14:17
[31] 1 Corinthians 4:20
[32] Matthew 11:12 ESV
[33] Philippians 4:11
[34] See John 12:24
[35] See Hosea 4:6
[36] 1 John 1:5
[37] Romans 8:19–21
[38] Matthew 10:7–8
[39] John 14:12
[40] John 5:19
[41] John 12:49
[42] Ephesians 5:17
[43] Colossians 1:9
[44] Matthew 18:14
[45] John 10:4–5, 27
[46] Isaiah 64:8
[47] Matthew 13:43
[48] Isaiah 29:13 and Matthew 15:8
[49] Hebrews 13:20–21
[50] Psalm 40:8
[51] Romans 12:2
[52] Revelation 1:6
[53] This quote is often misattributed to Yuri Gagarin as quoted in *To Rise from Earth* (1996) by Wayne Lee. According to Colonel Valentin Petrov, the quote originated from Nikita Kruschev's speech at the plenum of the Central Committee of the SPSU about the state's anti-religion campaign. Quotes: *YourDictionary* (March 19, 2016). Retrieved from http://quotes.yourdictionary.com/author/quote/603054.
[54] Revelation 12:3–9
[55] Isaiah 66:1
[56] Genesis 3:8
[57] Genesis 3:24
[58] Matthew 27:51
[59] Matthew 6:19–21
[60] Matthew 16:19

[61] Matthew 18:18–20
[62] Matthew 28:18–20
[63] John 6:66
[64] John 6:9–11
[65] Psalm 34:8
[66] John 3:30
[67] 2 Corinthians 12:9
[68] Luke 11:4
[69] Rabbi Mark Greenspan (March 19, 2016). *Please Can You Help Me Understand the Modern Meaning of the Word 'chayav'*. Retrieved from http://www.jewishvaluesonline.org/575.
[70] John 20:23 ESV
[71] Romans 6:23
[72] Matthew 18:23–35
[73] Romans 5:8
[74] NT:3986, *Thayer's Greek Lexicon*, Electronic Database. Copyright © 2000, 2003, 2006 by Biblesoft, Inc. All rights reserved.
[75] NT:3984, *Thayer's Greek Lexicon*, Electronic Database. Copyright © 2000, 2003, 2006 by Biblesoft, Inc. All rights reserved.
[76] John 10:10 ESV
[77] Exodus 16:4
[78] Psalm 26:2
[79] Psalm 44:21 and Matthew 6:8
[80] *dokimazo* (dok-im-ad'-zo); NT:1381, Biblesoft's *New Exhaustive Strong's Numbers and Concordance with Expanded Greek-Hebrew Dictionary*. Copyright © 1994, 2003, 2006 Biblesoft, Inc. and International Bible Translators, Inc.
[81] Matthew 26:41
[82] NT:4506, *Vine's Expository Dictionary of Biblical Words*, Copyright © 1985, Thomas Nelson Publishers.
[83] Ibid.
[84] Luke 1:74
[85] Colossians 1:13
[86] 2 Timothy 4:17–18
[87] NT:4190, *poneeros* (pon-ay-ros'), *Thayer's Greek Lexicon*, Electronic Database. Copyright © 2000, 2003, 2006 by Biblesoft, Inc. All rights reserved.
[88] Acts 19:12

[89] For more information on spiritual warfare and deliverance, see *Remedy: Freedom Through Deliverance* by Bill French and Michael French.
[90] 2 Corinthians 5:17
[91] Philippians 4:5 AMP
[92] NT:1933, *epieikees*, *Thayer's Greek Lexicon*, Electronic Database. Copyright © 2000, 2003, 2006 by Biblesoft, Inc. All rights reserved.
[93] Ephesians 5:15–16
[94] 1 Corinthians 10:16–17
[95] 1 Corinthians 12:12–27
[96] Psalm 46:1
[97] Hebrews 4:16
[98] Colossians 2:13–15
[99] 1 Timothy 4:7–9 and Hebrews 5:14
[100] John 8:44, Galatians 4:6–7, Romans 8:19–22
[101] Psalm 34:8
[102] NT:281, *Thayer's Greek Lexicon*, Electronic Database. Copyright © 2000, 2003, 2006 by Biblesoft, Inc. All rights reserved.
[103] 1 Peter 5:1

www.ingramcontent.com/pod-product-compliance
Lightning Source LLC
Chambersburg PA
CBHW021437080526
44588CB00009B/561